A *Letts* EXPLORE **Literature Guide**

First published 1994
Reprinted 1997

Letts Educational
Aldine House
Aldine Place
London W12 8AW
0181 740 2266

Text © John Mahoney and Stewart Martin 1994

This edition edited by Ron Simpson

Self-test questions devised by Claire Wright

Typeset by Jordan Publishing Design

Text design Jonathan Barnard

Cover illustration Ivan Allen

Text illustrations Hugh Marshall

Design © BPP (Letts Educational) Ltd

Acknowledgements
Every effort has been made to trace copyright holders and to obtain their permission for the use of copyright material. The author and publishers will gladly receive information enabling them to rectify any reference or credit in subsequent editions.

British Library Cataloguing in Publication Data
A CIP record for this book is available from the British Library

ISBN 1 85758 252 7

Printed and bound in Great Britain
Ashford Colour Press, Gosport, Hampshire

Letts Educational is the trading name of BPP (Letts Educational) Ltd

Contents

■ Plot synopsis

The action of the play is set in ancient Athens and in 'a wood near it'. The locations are very important in this play. Athens was traditionally 'the cradle of civilisation'. For Elizabethans it was where philosophy, logic and lawgiving began. In the play Athens represents a place of order, sanity and enlightenment. The wood, by contrast, is the home of nature and spirits. It is a place where things are often unpredictable, irrational and disordered, where people wander in and are changed from what they were, are lost and are found again. Some of the main concerns of the play are love, 'love-madness' and marriage. There are four different but related stories which run alongside each other and continually interconnect.

The first story is set in the human world. It begins with Theseus, the Duke of Athens, and Hippolyta who are looking forward to their forthcoming wedding. One of Theseus' subjects, Egeus, comes to him with a problem – his daughter Hermia refuses to marry the man he has chosen for her (Demetrius), because she loves another man, Lysander.

The second story starts here and is about the love tangles of four young lovers. Theseus tells Hermia she must do as her father says or be severely punished. Hermia runs away into the woods with her lover, Lysander. Before they escape they tell Helena what they are doing and why. Demetrius used to love Helena before he met Hermia. Helena still loves Demetrius and so she tells him about the planned escape, hoping by this to make him love her again. Helena's plan goes wrong. Demetrius pursues Hermia into the woods, and Helena follows him. The lovers get lost and separated in the woods.

At this point this first story meets the fourth story as Oberon, who is the King of the Fairies, sends his servant Puck to put a potion on the eyes of the sleeping Demetrius so that he will love Helena again. Puck puts it in the eyes of Lysander by mistake. As a result, when Lysander wakes up, he falls in love with Helena. To correct this mistake, Oberon puts the love-potion into the eyes of the sleeping Demetrius, who awakens and also falls in love with Helena. Now both Lysander and Demetrius declare their love for Helena but she becomes convinced that they are trying to make a fool of her. Helena and Hermia quarrel about who loves whom and the men prepare to fight a duel over Helena. Oberon tells Puck to sort out the mess and make all well again, which he does. Theseus arrives and says the four lovers should marry whomever they wish.

The third story is about a group of workmen who are rehearsing a play to be performed at the wedding of Theseus and Hippolyta. Their amateurish attempts to rehearse their play are amusing. They rehearse in the woods away from the public gaze because their play is not ready to be seen. Oberon sends his servant Puck to put a special love-potion on the eyes of his sleeping Queen, Titania, as a punishment for a her disobedience. When Titania wakes up she will fall in love with the first thing she sees. Puck also finds the workmen rehearsing their play and mischievously changes the head one of them, Bottom, into that of an ass. Bottom accidentally wakens the sleeping Titania and she falls in love with him. After being entertained for a time in the spirit world, Bottom is returned to normal by Puck, who also removes the love-potion from the eyes of Titania. Bottom thinks he has had a wonderful dream. The workmen's play is performed as planned at the wedding of Theseus and Hippolyta and the four lovers are married at the same time.

The fourth story is set in the woods, in the world of spirits, and is about Oberon and his Queen, Titania. They quarrel about which of them owns a servant boy. In anger, Oberon decides to put a special potion on Titania's eyes while she sleeps, so on awakening she will love the first thing she sees. Oberon also decides to turn the tables on the human lover, Demetrius, by having some of this potion put on his eyes, so he will love Helena. Oberon's plans go comically wrong when his servant Puck confuses the two lovers. Puck also mischievously gives one of the workmen, Bottom, the head of an ass and Titania falls in love with him when she awakens. Eventually Puck is ordered by Oberon to restore everything to the way it was and the story ends happily with Oberon blessing the marriages of Theseus and Hippolyta and the four lovers.

Different editions of a Shakespeare play are usually very similar, although they may show occasional variation in spelling, punctuation and the arrangement of the lines. You may even come across differences in act or scene divisions but you should not find any difficulty in identifying the particular point or section being commented on in this Guide. The quotations and comments in this Guide are referenced to the Penguin edition of the play.

Who's who in
A Midsummer Night's Dream

The lovers

The lovers

The four young lovers are Demetrius, Lysander, Helena and Hermia. They behave as individuals in the play. They also act as a group, when they represent the theme of young love. They are from aristocratic families.

Demetrius, having thrown over Helena, is in love with Hermia. During the play he has a love-potion put in his eyes which makes him love Helena again. At the end of the play he marries Helena.

Lysander is also in love with Hermia and runs away with her. During the play he has a love-potion put in his eyes that makes him love Helena and he cruelly rejects Hermia. Later the potion is removed and he marries Hermia.

Helena is unhappy and rejected at the start of the play. She and Demetrius used to be lovers, but he has now fallen in love with Hermia. She is a rather unhappy figure throughout the play and even at the end is unsure about her sudden good fortune, when she marries Demetrius, who now loves her again because of the love-potion.

At the start of the play Hermia disobeys her father Egeus by refusing to marry Demetrius. Instead she runs away into the woods with her lover, Lysander. Hermia has a happier time of it than Helena. She is also physically smaller (shorter) than Helena and this provides comedy in Act 3 Sc 2. At the end of the play she marries Lysander.

Oberon

Oberon

Oberon is the King of the Fairies. He has great magical powers and is the dominant figure in the world of fairies and spirits. His influence permeates the play. He is jealous and vindictive when aroused as, for example, when Titania refuses to hand over the changeling boy to him. It is his revenge on her and his unpredictable meddling in the tangled love affairs of the humans in the wood which leads to the comic misunderstanding and confusion in the middle scenes of the play. He is also active in the human world. Titania says he 'steals away from fairy land' to 'the farthest steep of India'. She also accuses him of a past affair with Theseus' bride, Hippolyta. He shows his better side when he relents and releases Titania from the spell. At the end of the play, Oberon and Titania hold the stage as the guardian spirits, showering blessings on the three sleeping married couples.

Titania

Titania

Titania is Oberon's queen and in many ways his equal. She is described throughout the play as a supremely beautiful woman who is graceful and sensuous. As she makes clear, her refusal to return the boy to Oberon is only out of regard for the memory of her friendship with the boy's dead mother. After her bewitchment by her husband's love potion, her scenes with Bottom are, at one and the same time, charming, sensual and comic. She too is active in the human world. Oberon accuses her of having had an affair with Theseus. At the end of the play Oberon and Titania settle their quarrel and are reunited in their loving relationship. This gives the play a sense of completeness.

Puck

Puck

Puck is Oberon's mischievous servant, who loves especially to play pranks on humans. He is not very reliable or efficient at carrying out instructions and the confusion among the four human lovers is caused by his mistakes with the love-potion. Puck never feels regret for his pranks and practical jokes. His character is based on a traditional folklore figure called Robin Goodfellow.

In performance Puck is presented in many different ways. Often a very physical character, with mime as important as speech, he is also frequently played in 'naughty schoolboy' style. For a clue to Shakespeare's idea of the character, you might look at 'I jest to Oberon' in Act 2 Sc 1.

The workmen

The workmen, who all have amusing names, behave as a group who act together in the play, with the exception of Bottom, who is a much more developed character than any of the others.

As a group, the workmen represent the clumsy sincerity of the 'rude mechanicals' (simple, ordinary folk). Their attempts to put on a noble and sophisticated play for the wedding of Theseus (ruler of Athens) and Hippolyta are ludicrous, but their laborious literal-mindedness is also genuine and touching.

Flute is a bellows-mender who, reluctantly, plays the woman's part in the play.

Snout is a tinker who is given the part of the Wall in the play.

Snug, a dim-witted joiner, has the part of the Lion, which consists only of roaring. He is, nonetheless, worried about remembering his 'lines'!

Starveling is a tailor who is given the part of Moonshine in the play and is notable for the amusing way he loses patience with the courtiers who laugh at his final performance.

Peter Quince, the carpenter, is the play's director and, with the possible exception of Nick Bottom, the most human and 'real' of the mechanicals. Where most seem ignorant or apprehensive, Quince is ambitious and doggedly pursues his production despite his failings and those of his cast. His attempts to discipline and teach his players are farcical, as is his mispunctuated Prologue, but it is not difficult to sympathise with him when the aristocrats mock his efforts.

Bottom, a weaver, is the most wildly enthusiastic and self-confident of all the workmen in the play. He would happily play all the parts himself, if the other workmen would let him! He is good-natured, honest and innocent and has difficulty telling reality from illusion. Oberon's servant Puck plays a mischievous prank on Bottom and magically gives him the head of an ass. When Oberon's queen Titania awakens the love-potion in her eyes makes her fall in love with the transformed Bottom. Finally returning to normal, Bottom quickly forgets his 'dream' and the workmen's play goes ahead as planned.

Theseus, Duke of Athens

Theseus is the embodiment of Athens and its strict rule of law. Nonetheless, conscious of his own happiness with Hippolyta, he shows understanding to Hermia at the start of the play and kindness and consideration towards all the lovers at the end. His forthcoming marriage seems to set the mood of tolerance and forgiveness, towards which the play always seems to be moving. He is, in part, a mirror to Oberon, showing by contrast how power can be used wisely and responsibly.

It is now quite common for productions to use two actors doubling Theseus/Oberon and Hippolyta/Titania, thus emphasising the way the fairy world mirrors the Athenian court. It should, of course, be clear that Shakespeare's Athens bears little resemblance to the world of Ancient Greece. The marriage of Theseus and the Amazon queen occurs in Greek myth, but the supernatural figures he was used to dealing with were gods and monsters, not fairies. Also Quince, Bottom and their colleagues hardly seem Athenian: to what time and society do you think they belong?

Hippolyta

Hippolyta is the defeated Queen of the Amazons, who is to marry Theseus. She is, perhaps, an example of wildness tamed, first by power, and then by the influence of civilisation. She is given little to say, but in the final scenes she shows a lively sympathy with the lovers.

Egeus

Egeus is the father of Hermia. He is a rather unloving, narrow-minded and fussy kind of authority figure and the oldest human character in the play. His demand for the strict letter of the law strikes a discordant note early in the play. Eventually Theseus overrules him and he disappears from the action.

Themes and images in *A Midsummer Night's Dream*

> **Themes** are the important ideas that run through the play. You will come across them many times. They connect the story, the characters and the different scenes in the play.
>
> When words and descriptions suggest a picture in your mind, that is called an **image**. Images are often used to make an idea stronger, or to encourage you to think of things from a particular point of view. If you described someone as being 'as thin as a rake' or as behaving 'like a wild animal' you would be using simple examples of images.
>
> Shakespeare was a great writer who used themes and images all the time. Many of the examples you will find are very striking and impressive. Other examples will be less obvious, so you will need to pay careful attention to the language that Shakespeare has used. Read the following notes carefully.

Illusion

Illusion

The imagination is so powerful that it can sometimes create illusions that seem more real than life itself. The play uses this idea to raise questions about what is 'real' to people. Often the play uses occasions when characters are asleep to explore the way dreams can sometimes seem as real and believable as everyday life. There are ten occasions when seven different characters are asleep on stage, with three of these characters falling asleep twice. The play also emphasises the importance of imagination by stressing how the audience must use their imagination to give the play itself life and by showing how the workmen's drama requires the other characters in the play to use their imagination, if it is to be successful.

Most of the play (from Act 2 Sc 1 to Act 4 Sc 1) takes place in the wood during a single night, in which the characters exist in one long 'dream' or illusion, until the Duke's hunting party arrives, bringing the dawn and the return of sanity. Most of the 'falling asleep and waking' is there to serve the requirements of the plot.

Love

Love

The play emphasises the difference between 'real', i.e. mature love, and 'doting' or 'infatuation', which is love with no basis in reality. Mature love is shown as involving not only raw passion and emotion but also thoughtfulness and forgiveness. Marriage is shown as its proper outcome. The quarrel between Oberon and Titania is used to show how the harmony of the world of nature is disturbed by any upset in their relationship. True love leads to harmony, but discord and chaos result when lovers quarrel.

Moon

Moon

The moon exerts a powerful influence through the imagery of the play. Time is measured for all characters by the moon and its power over large parts of the world, like the tides, is often stressed. The world, illuminated by the moon, is portrayed as cold and fruitless, and the moon's power is shown as mysterious. Most of the action takes place at night and the moon or moonlight are mentioned in this play three times more often than in all Shakespeare's other plays together.

Nature

Nature

The world of nature is shown as vibrant and bursting with life and activity, even when to humans it seems asleep. The spirits in the play are the most powerful expression of the forces hidden within the natural world. The most beautiful example of this is in Act 2 Sc 1, where Titania's bower is described. The love-potion, which plays such an important part in the story, is distilled from nature and is an example of the mysterious powers that are hidden in the natural world. This theme is closely connected with the way the moon is used as another mysterious and ambiguous force in nature. The colours of nature are often mentioned in connection with birds, flowers, fruit, the eyes and lips of young women, the dawn and the many animals and insects which are described in the play.

Order

Order

The action of the play begins with discord and ends with the restoration of order. The people of Shakespeare's time (the Elizabethans) saw order throughout the world of nature and for them it was an important and respected idea. The order in the natural world should, according to the Elizabethans, be echoed by a respect for order in the world of humans, with proper concern being shown for all forms of order and authority. The Elizabethans thought that without order in the world chaos would reign. At the opening of the play Theseus has to deal with a father whose daughter is rebelling against his authority. The ordered relationship between Oberon and Titania is also under threat because of their quarrel. The four young lovers eventually arrive at a harmonious and ordered situation (marriage), but only after the play has shown how disruptive and damaging their arguments and squabbles can be. Even the 'most lamentable comedy' of the workmen's struggle to perform their play demonstrates how disruptive disorder can be. Music is used in the play along with dancing and singing as symbolic of happiness, harmony and order. The occasions when these appear increase in number as the play nears its end, as the action moves from the discord and chaos at the beginning to the harmony and order of the conclusion.

Essays

This icon is used throughout the **Text commentary** to draw attention to material that should be of particular relevance to the section **How to write a coursework essay**. Each time it is used, it is accompanied by a note that identifies which essay title the material relates to and adds a relevant comment, quotation or piece of advice.

■ Text commentary

Act 1 Scene 1

Theseus, Duke of Athens, is arranging to celebrate his marriage with Hippolyta, Queen of the Amazons, whom he has recently defeated in battle. Egeus arrives and complains that his daughter Hermia will not obey his wish for her to marry Demetrius, because Lysander has bewitched her into loving him instead. Theseus warns Hermia that if she does not obey her father he must condemn her to death or to life as a nun. Hermia and Lysander decide to elope. Hermia's friend Helena tells Demetrius of Hermia's plans.

Love

The play begins in a quiet and romantic mood as Theseus and Hippolyta discuss their forthcoming wedding. The love of Theseus and Hippolyta is shown as at once passionate and restrained. They are looking forward to their wedding in four days' time but are able to exercise self-control. Marriage is shown as an important event, full of happiness and celebration.

Moon

The significance of the moon is established at once, being mentioned three times in the first ten lines of the play and over thirty times before the play ends. Its influence is predominant throughout the play. This opening scene is one of the very few in the play that happens in daylight.

Notice that Theseus says the relationship between himself and Hippolyta began in conflict and discord: 'I woo'd thee with my sword, and won thy love doing thee injuries'. This pattern is followed by all the relationships in the play. Each relationship in the play begins or has begun in discord, chaos or conflict.

The entry of the angry Egeus marks a sudden change of mood. Such contrasts of mood and character happen a lot in the play and help to make the story more varied and interesting.

Egeus is angry with his daughter Hermia

Illusion

Egeus is angry because he has given Demetrius permission to marry his daughter Hermia but says that another man, Lysander, has 'bewitched' her, so that she now wants to marry him instead. Egeus says that Lysander has used songs and moonlight as well as poetry, gifts, the exchange of locks of hair and other kinds of 'feigning' (pretending) of his affections to 'filch' (steal) his daughter's love. The idea that people's feelings can be influenced by magic, songs and moonlight so that they can not tell what is real and become 'bewitched' is introduced right at the start of the play.

Egeus is here the stock figure of age and authority demanding obedience from the young. In Shakespeare's time children were expected to obey their parents more than is often the case today. This is why Theseus says that Hermia should treat her father like 'a god'.

Theseus passes judgement

There is a very real conflict here between the right of a woman to marry the

Order

man she loves and the right of a father to control his daughter's behaviour. From the law she can expect death and from her father a life married to a man she doesn't love. Theseus is the ruler of Athens and he must see that the laws are obeyed, but he can sympathise with Hermia because he is in love himself. His wisdom is shown when he tells Hermia to think the

matter over carefully and postpones his decision until the next new moon, which is the day of his own wedding. This is Theseus being used as the 'wise ruler' in the play in the same way that Egeus is being used as the 'angry father'.

Love

Theseus cautions Hermia to consider her answer carefully. He says that if she disobeys her father she must either face the death penalty or become a nun. He says her youth will make it difficult for her to be a nun and live her life as a 'barren sister' (meaning she will have no children), spending her time 'chanting faint hymns to the cold fruitless moon'.

Order

Demetrius begs Hermia to change her mind and marry him as her father wishes. Lysander says that Hermia should marry him because they are in love. In any case, says Lysander, Demetrius already loves someone else and this other woman – Helena – also loves Demetrius. Theseus agrees that he has also heard this to be true and he takes Demetrius and Egeus

off for 'some private schooling'. Theseus clearly recognises that there are two sides to this argument and the word 'schooling' is nicely ambiguous. Theseus may have taken the two men aside to give them some private advice or he may have done so in order to tell them off.

Characters

The only scene between a pair of lovers before the madness takes over: what can you learn of their feelings? And a very appropriate quotation: 'The course of true love never did run smooth'.

Hermia and Lysander decide to run away

When everyone else has left the stage, the two lovers have a private conversation. Lysander tries to cheer up Hermia and tells her that 'the course of true love never did run smooth', which is a central theme of the play. The lovers talk about all the things that seem to go wrong with the course of true love – how lovers are often from very different levels in society ('too high to be enthrall'd to low') or of very different ages ('misgraffed in respect of years'). Notice how the two lovers speak one after the other line-by-line to emphasise that they share the same feelings. Lysander uses images of shadows and light to emphasise the way love seems fleeting so that 'ere a man hath power to say "Behold!", the jaws of darkness do devour it up'. Their conversation is quite sad and Hermia describes their love as 'cross'd' (destined to have bad luck). Lysander tells her he has a rich, widowed aunt living seven leagues away who, being childless, treats him as her own son. He suggests that the law of Athens cannot reach them there and they should therefore go there and be married. They agree to meet in the wood outside the town the following night and then run away together.

The wood

The wood where Hermia and Lysander agree to meet has a large part to play in *A Midsummer Night's Dream*. All the main characters in the play gather in this wood, which is a place of darkness, danger, mystery, magic and unreality. It is in the wood that the lovers' feelings for each other are tested. It is in this wood that the worlds of the impossible and the real collide and blur into each other. In Elizabethan times the word 'wood' also had the meaning 'mad'.

Illusion

About the language

Hermia's speech 'I swear to thee by Cupid's strongest bow...' marks a change of language in this scene. From this point to the end it is in rhyming couplets. Rhyming couplets give what is said a rather stiff and artificial feeling. This is deliberate: rhyming couplets lift the language out of the ordinary, emphasising the special quality of what is being said. Here the lovers pledge their love to each other. This way of writing can also suggest that what the characters say should not be taken too seriously, because they are speaking in rather formal and flowery language. This was a familiar theatrical device in Shakespeare's day and the audience would have quickly recognised it. You will notice that this device is similar to one you have already met in which Hermia and Lysander each spoke a line of a couplet in turn to show how they shared the same feelings and had sympathy for each other. Here, this kind of link is further emphasised by the way Hermia's and Helena's words echo each other in patterns, as when they are talking about Demetrius, and Hermia says: 'The more I hate, the more he follows me', to which Helena replies: 'The more I love, the more he hateth me.'

Helena is told about the lovers' plans to elope

Hermia and Lysander tell Helena about the way they plan to run away,

Moon

although a rather ironic and ominous tone is sounded when Hermia says they will escape through the wood at midnight 'to seek new friends, and stranger companies'. This is ironic because Hermia speaks more than she knows. The lovers are indeed going to find strange company in the woods. Notice the way Lysander's speech is full of references to the watchful Phoebe (the moon goddess) and the way her light transforms the ordinary world into a place of great strangeness and beauty, 'decking with liquid pearl the bladed grass'. Throughout the play there is a suggestion that the moon and its light have a mysterious power and influence over people. The moon and its light even seem to have some influence over the passage of time and over what is real and unreal.

Helena decides that she will tell Demetrius of the escape plan

The lovers

Illusion

Helena speaks the first soliloquy in the play. A soliloquy is a speech in which a character reveals to the audience his or her inner thoughts. Helena is the female character who will suffer most before the end of the play. She also outlines an important theme of the play, that love can rob people of their common sense so that they see things the way they wish to see them rather than as they really are. She says this is why Cupid is always shown as blindfolded. Knowing this does not stop people from falling in love, however, and Helena loves Demetrius even though he treats her terribly.

Helena sums this up when she says:

'Things base and vile, holding no quantity,
Love can transpose to form and dignity:
Love looks not with the eyes, but with the mind,
And therefore is wing'd Cupid painted blind.'

Characters
'How happy some o'er other some can be!'/'herein mean I to enrich my pain'. How far do these lines sum up Helena?

She decides to tell Demetrius about Lysander and Hermia's planned elopement because she knows that Demetrius will then pursue Hermia to the woods the following night. She says that she doesn't care what it costs, just so long as it makes Demetrius pay her some attention again.

Act 1 Scene 2

The workmen meet to rehearse the play they are to perform at the wedding of Theseus and Hippolyta.

The workmen assemble and Quince, the carpenter, tells them that their play

will be *Pyramus and Thisbe*. This is a famous classical love story (which in some ways echoes the story of *A Midsummer Night's Dream*). In keeping with the change of atmosphere from the last scene, notice how this scene has switched from verse back into prose.

The workmen

Bottom, the weaver, is typically enthusiastic about everything, keeps butting in, and says finally that, although he will happily play the part of Pyramus (a lover), he would really prefer to play a tyrant. Although Bottom's puppy-like enthusiasm is amusing, what he says contains a truth hidden to him, for the role of love in *A Midsummer Night's Dream* will indeed be that of a kind of tyrant.

The humour in this scene comes from the way the unsophisticated workmen take themselves very seriously. By describing the ludicrous and over-enthusiastic 'ham' acting methods they will use, they show the audience that the performance of a classical play is completely beyond them.

Order

Even the full title of the play they will do is a mixture of comedy and tragedy: *The Most Lamentable Comedy and Most Cruel Death of Pyramus and Thisbe*. This play reflects the mixture of comedy and sadness that occurs in *A Midsummer Night's Dream*.

Humour

Low comedy: Bottom's attempt at a speech in 'Ercles' vein'; his ambition to play all parts; Quince's gross flattery to persuade him otherwise; misunderstandings and mangling of English all round.

Bottom is determined to play as many parts as possible and will go to any lengths to convince his friends that he can do so. In reply to their worries that if he were the lion he would roar too fiercely, he says he would 'roar as gently as any sucking dove' or 'any nightingale'! After Quince has finally

Illusion

established that Bottom cannot play all the parts himself and will play only Pyramus, the chatterbox Bottom immediately starts to worry about what kind of beard he should wear. Flute protests that he doesn't want to play the woman because he has a beard coming, but Quince tells him he will be wearing a mask and may speak 'small' (in thin tones), so no one will know it is him. Quince tells everyone to learn their lines for the next night. They are to meet at the Duke's oak in the wood outside the town to rehearse in private. This is the same wood where the lovers Hermia and Lysander plan to meet to begin their escape. Again the wood is to play a part in secret meetings. Notice also that, illuminated by moonlight, it is to be the location for the creation of illusion (the workmen's play).

Athens or England?

Often in Shakespeare's plays the common people are presented as English men and women of the sixteenth century despite the setting in Italy, Denmark, Greece or wherever else. In this case there is no suggestion of the Ancient Greek about the mechanicals: the names and the reference to France are two obvious indications of their Englishness. You might also note the use of 'interlude' (a type of play popular in Tudor England) in the opening lines. The best joke, however, is that Bottom, who misuses language throughout, gets the names of Greek gods and heroes wrong: who do you think Ercles and Phibbus are?

Discord and disharmony

The ideas of discord, conflict and disharmony are introduced at the start of the play. Theseus first met Hippolyta in battle; Egeus enters in fury at his daughter Hermia's disobedience; Lysander and Hermia are lovers who are forced apart; Helena's love for Demetrius is not returned by him; the workmen's arrangements for the play are chaotic; and in Act 2 Puck tells us that Oberon and Titania have quarrelled. Theseus's comment about winning someone's love by doing them injury applies to all these relationships in one way or another. Mature and aristocratic authority is shown as restrained and wise, whilst immature young love is shown as fickle. The young lovers will change and re-change their minds about each other during the course of the play. The conflict between obedience to authority and individual desire, and the dangers it can lead to, have been introduced with Hermia disobeying her father Egeus and risking death and, at a more comic level, as the workmen worry that Bottom's behaviour will frighten the ladies of the Duke's court, wreck the play, and get them all hanged.

Self-test questions Act 1

Uncover the plot
Delete two of the three alternatives given, to find the correct plot. Beware possible misconceptions and muddles.

Theseus and Hippolyta/Hermia/Helena look forward to their wedding at the new moon/full moon/half moon. Egeus complains that his daughter Hermia/Helena/Hippolyta refuses to marry Lysander/Demetrius/Philostrate, because she is in love with Lysander/Demetrius/Philostrate. (Demetrius was previously in love with Hermia/Helena/Hippolyta.) If disobedient, Hermia must choose death or marriage to another/banishment from Athens/life as a nun. The lovers complain that 'true lovers have been ever smooth/cross/cross'd' and decide to escape to a house one/seven/six leagues from Athens. Helena wishes she was like Hippolyta/Hermia/Titania: Hermia assures her she does not want Lysanders'/Demetrius'/Egeus' love – indeed she is escaping. Helena resolves to tell Theseus/Egeus/Demetrius of their plan. Meanwhile, under the direction of Bottom/Quince/Snout, the workmen prepare a play: Bottom/Quince/Snout is to play Pyramus, with Snug/Starveling/Flute as Thisbe.

Who? What? Where? Why? How?
1 Who is to be married in four days' time? (Give their full titles)
2 Who is to play the lion – and who wants to?
3 What three arguments does Lysander present to Theseus in his and Hermia's favour?
4 What three styles of writing are used in this Act: when, and to what effect?
5 Where do the lovers plan to escape to?
6 Where is this Act set?
7 Why does Helena tell Demetrius of Hermia's plan?
8 Why do the workmen not want Bottom to play the lion?
9 How, according to Egeus, has Lysander 'bewitched' Hermia?
10 How have Theseus and Hippolyta met?

Who said that?
1 Who says: 'As she is mine I may dispose of her' and of whom?
2 Who says: 'Or else the law of Athens yields you up – /Which by no means we may extenuate'?
3 Who says: 'Things base and vile, holding no quantity/Love can transpose to form and dignity'?
4 Who says: 'Making it momentary as a sound/Swift as a shadow, short as any dream' and of what?
5 Who says: 'We will meet; and there we may rehearse most obscenely and courageously'?

Open quotes
Find the line – and complete the phrase or sentence.
1 'Hippolyta, I woo'd thee with my sword...'
2 'And she, sweet lady, dotes...'
3 'Ay me! for aught that I could ever read...'
4 'The more I hate, the more he follows me...' (Hermia)
5 'Love looks not with the eyes...'

Connections

There are several different 'worlds' and plot strands in the play: royals, lovers, workmen, fairies. They are all interconnected. Let's explore.

1 What connections are made between the various plot stands in the play by the following?
   Theseus says: 'Awake the pert and nimble spirit of mirth'
   Lysander, talking of doomed love, says: 'So quick bright things come to confusion'
   Hermia says they will 'seek new friends and stranger companies'
2 Who agrees to meet in the wood, outside the town on the following night?
3 Where are the workmen to perform their play?

Lunacy

The word 'lunacy' comes from 'luna' – the moon, which was supposed to have strange effects on people. Moonlight is very important in the play. Let's explore.

1 In what context does Theseus first mention the moon?
2 What image does Hippolyta use to describe the new moon, and why is this apt?
3 Who has sung by moonlight – and who will chant hymns to the 'cold fruitless moon'?
4 What image does Lysander use for the moon's reflection on the ocean?
5 What lighting is the workmen's rehearsal to have?

Act 2 Scene 1

Puck and a fairy discuss the conflict between Oberon, King of the Fairies and Titania, his Fairy Queen. Titania refuses to give Oberon a young boy and leaves. Oberon orders Puck to fetch the special flower from which he will make a love-potion to put in Titania's sleeping eyes. This will make her fall in love with the first thing she sees on awakening. Oberon overhears Demetrius being unkind to Helena and vows to put the potion in the eyes of Demetrius also. Puck returns with the flower and is sent with some of the potion to find Demetrius. Oberon takes the rest of the potion and goes to look for Titania.

At the start of this scene the fairy sings the first of the play's five songs, all of

Puck

which are written in rhyme. Puck tells the fairy the background to the quarrel between Oberon and Titania. The argument is about an Indian boy – a 'changeling' boy, meaning a fairy child – and has reached such intensity that 'their elves for fear creep into acorn-cups, and hide them there'. The fairy talks about all the kinds of pranks for which Puck is known. Puck's mischief is unplanned and exists for no reason other than the amusement it gives him.

'Ill met by moonlight, proud Titania'

Moon

Order

With these words Oberon greets Titania and they emphasise the importance of moonlight as the setting for events in the fairy world. They also summarise the situation of the lovers when they enter the wood.

The conversation between Oberon and Titania shows that even supernatural beings sometimes squabble like jealous lovers. This strengthens the link between the world of the fairies and the world of the humans and is emphasised when Oberon accuses Titania of a past romance with Theseus and she accuses him of having a secret attraction to Hippolyta. This section of the play establishes Oberon and Titania as *adults*, whose actions *matter* to the world. Puck and the fairies are closer to childhood.

Imagery, language and verse

A wonderfully evocative opening line, 'Ill met by moonlight, proud Titania'. Note all the adjectives of decay: their jealous quarrel casts a spell over the world.

Nature

Titania lists all the things that have gone wrong in the world of nature since their quarrel began: there have been terrible fogs, the rivers have overflowed and have rotted the crops and filled everywhere with mud; the moon's light now 'washes all the air' so that 'rheumatic diseases do abound' and frost and winter seem to have come early to the earth. The disturbance in the fairies' world has affected the world of humans. Oberon replies that all he wants is the changeling boy, but Titania refuses; the boy is the son of one of her mortal friends and she is going to look after him. Titania leaves with her fairy attendants.

Oberon vows to torment Titania

Oberon

Because he cannot have the changeling boy, Oberon says he will punish Titania for refusing him. He takes her refusal as an 'injury' or insult, but notice how this echoes Theseus' use of the word ('won thy love doing thee injuries'). Oberon then tells Puck about the plant which he wants him to go and find.

Oberon's speech is full of references to wonderful and magical things. He is more powerful than Puck and can see things in the spirit world that Puck cannot, such as Cupid 'flying between the cold moon and

Moon

the earth'. He reminds Puck of the time he saw a mermaid's singing calm a rough sea and made stars shoot across the sky. The reference to a mermaid is interesting because later in the play Bottom is turned into a half-human, half-animal being.

Imagery, language and verse

Classical imagery (Cupid, 'fair vestal', 'imperial votaress') side by side with Puck's striking image ('put a girdle round the earth') for his speed of travel.

A compliment to Queen Elizabeth I

Love

Queen Elizabeth I was on the throne when Shakespeare wrote this play. She publicly prided herself on remaining a virgin and the reference in Oberon's speech to 'a fair vestal' is almost certainly a flattering reference to her. In Roman mythology virgin priestesses tended the shrine of Vesta, the goddess of the hearth. Oberon says that Cupid tried to shoot an arrow 'at a fair vestal, throned by the west'. Cupid was the Roman god of love, represented as a winged boy with a bow and arrow.

Love-in-idleness

Nature

Illusion

Cupid's arrow missed its mark and instead hit a small flower, making it change from white to purple. Because the arrow did not hit something capable of feeling love, its power remained trapped – or 'idle' – in the flower. This is why Oberon calls the flower 'love-in-idleness'. Squeezing its juice on to the eyes of sleeping mortals makes them fall in love with the first living thing they see when they awaken. The common name of this flower is the pansy, but Oberon's description of it makes it sound magical.

Puck leaves, saying he will 'put a girdle round about the earth in forty minutes', emphasising how swiftly he will obey Oberon's instructions. In a soliloquy, Oberon tells how he will put the juice of the flower in the eyes of Titania while she sleeps. He wants her to wake up and fall in love with some wild creature such as a lion, a bear, a wolf, a bull, a monkey or an ape and says he will make her give him the changeling boy before he removes the 'charm' (magic) from her sight with another herb which he knows of. The audience thus knows from the start that Oberon intends to release Titania from the charm eventually and so can relax and enjoy the unfolding of the comedy.

A note about characters in the play and Shakespeare's use of soliloquy

In *A Midsummer Night's Dream* Shakespeare did not use soliloquy as much as he did in many of his other plays. A soliloquy is a very good way of letting the audience see into a character's thoughts. Because the audience is given so few soliloquies in this play, it will tend to see the characters less as individuals and more as 'types'. You should already be aware of this in the case of Theseus, who is shown as 'the wise ruler'; or Egeus, as 'the angry parent'; and

Puck

Puck, who is shown as 'the mischievous sprite'. As the action of the play moves into the wood, this trend becomes even more noticeable. The lovers themselves seem not to recognise each other and become confused about who loves whom. The characters in A Midsummer Night's Dream are best seen as representatives of an idea as theme and as 'types' rather than as fully rounded dramatic characters whom we feel we get to know as individuals. Shakespeare is dealing very much with 'stock' characters in this play. Even the memorable Bottom is something of a caricature.

Now back to the story

Because Oberon is invisible to mortals, he can eavesdrop on their

Illusion

conversation. Demetrius has come into the wood looking for Hermia, having been told of the lovers' escape plan by Helena, who, in turn, has followed him. Demetrius is angry because he cannot find Hermia and Lysander. Notice Demetrius' play on the word 'wood', which in those days could also mean 'mad', when he says he is 'wood within this wood'. This anticipates the way reality and madness will become confused in the wood, as the magical world of the spirits takes hold of the imagination so that characters cannot tell what is real and what is unreal.

Characters

The first long scene with Demetrius. What sort of a person does he seem? 'I love thee not, therefore pursue me not'/'I am sick when I do look on thee'/'I'll ... leave thee to the mercy of wild beasts.'

The lovers

Demetrius tells Helena that she is not to follow him any more and that he does not love her, but she replies that she loves him so much that she will follow him no matter how badly he treats her. This shows how love can change behaviour, a point made elsewhere in the play.

Helena says she will reverse the normal course of things and chase after Demetrius. She pictures the dove chasing the griffin, an imaginary animal with the head of an eagle and the body of a lion. This is another reference to fabulous beasts – like Oberon's mention of a mermaid – that anticipates the way Bottom is changed. It foreshadows the way other things will be turned back-to-front in the wood. Oberon sympathises with her and declares that before Demetrius leaves the wood, it will be he who pursues Helena.

'I know a bank where the wild thyme blows'

Puck

Nature

This line begins Oberon's instructions to Puck, who has returned with the flower. Puck is told that Oberon will put the flower's juice into the eyes of the sleeping Titania, whilst he is to find Demetrius and do the same to him. He will know the man by his Athenian clothes. Neither Puck nor Oberon knows that Lysander and Hermia will also be coming into the wood.

Oberon's description of Titania's bower, or sleeping place, is full of beautiful references to the profusion of nature. It conjures up a sweet and drowsy feeling with words like 'luscious' and 'nodding'. Descriptions of nature in the play, like this one here, reinforce the magic and beauty of the faries' world.

Imagery, language and verse

Possibly the most beautiful use of flower imagery ('nodding violet', 'luscious woodbine', 'sweet musk-roses', etc.) as part of the fairy world.

Act 2 Scene 2

Oberon finds the sleeping Titania and puts potion in her eyes. The exhausted Lysander and Hermia enter and fall asleep. Puck enters, mistakes Lysander for Demetrius and puts the potion in his eyes. Demetrius appears, chased by Helena, but he shakes her off and goes on alone. Lysander awakes, sees Helena and falls in love with her. Helena is upset by this sudden change towards her and leaves, pursued by Lysander. Hermia awakens to find herself alone.

Songs are important in *A Midsummer Night's Dream* and here the song 'You spotted snakes with double tongue' is a dramatic device to make Titania fall asleep so that Oberon can enter and put the flower juice into her eyes. The singing, dancing and music add to the fairy-like quality of the scene. Notice that Oberon speaks in rhyming couplets which gives his words a particular chanting rhythm, like a magical incantation. There are seven syllables to each line: the Elizabethans thought seven was a magic number.

Puck puts flower juice in the eyes of the sleeping Lysander

The lovers

Love

When Lysander and Hermia arrive, Lysander admits that they are lost. As they lie down to sleep Hermia asks him to lie down some way away from her, out of respect for her virtue. Lysander's protestations of innocence and Hermia's insistence that he behave himself are amusing. Before they fall asleep, they promise to remain in love with each other to the ends of their lives. This is ironic because when Puck arrives he thinks that Lysander is Demetrius, the 'disdainful youth' whom Oberon told him about. Puck assumes that, because he is dressed in Athenian clothes – 'weeds of Athens', as he calls them – he is the man he has been told to find. Puck puts the flower juice in the eyes of Lysander and departs, not realising his mistake. The audience will appreciate how this makes a nonsense of the vow of love that Lysander and Hermia swore just before they fell asleep. Notice that Puck also speaks in rhyming couplets. The use of rhyming couplets creates a feeling of 'distance' from natural speech and is therefore appropriate for supernatural beings to use.

Helena and Demetrius arrive

Illusion

At this point Helena and Demetrius run in, she chasing him. Helena has to pause because she is out of breath and Demetrius escapes. She is sad and says she must be 'as ugly as a bear', because 'beasts' that meet her run away in fright. By beasts she is thinking not of wild animals but of the 'monster', Demetrius. She sees Lysander asleep on the ground but doesn't see Hermia lying asleep some way off. When Lysander is woken up by Helena, he instantly falls in love with her because of the love-potion in his eyes.

Characters

From 'Transparent Helena!' onwards, the lovers as a group have no control over their emotions, both loving and aggressive: already Lysander is talking of a duel with Demetrius!

Lysander says he loves Helena and rejects Hermia

Love

Lysander makes a wild and exaggerated speech here about how much he loves Helena. Notice how he says his love is based on 'reason' (logic). This is ironic because the audience knows that his love is caused by the magic charm from the flower juice which has put reason aside. Lysander is finding logical excuses for his completely irrational behaviour. Helena thinks that Lysander is taunting her and considers his vows of love to her to be 'keen mockery', which she does not deserve. She leaves in disgust.

Dreams and the truth

Lysander is left alone with the sleeping Hermia. He tells her sleeping figure

Illusion

that he hates her. He leaves her and goes off to follow Helena. Hermia awakens in panic from a bad dream. She has dreamt that a serpent was eating away at her heart whilst Lysander sat smiling and looking on. In a way her dream is true, another illustration of the way dreams have the power to reveal the truth in a way that reality cannot. Hermia runs off to look for Lysander. The still-sleeping Titania is left alone.

The power of dreams to reveal the truth is demonstrated in the case of Hermia and a hint given that the world of dreams and the imagination is as full of frightening images as the woods are full of frightening animals.

The use of language

There are more examples of the **use of language** in the play. The language which the lovers use to each other when they are in love is different from the language they use when they are not. Compare, for example, the ornate, exaggerated rhyming couplets that Lysander uses with Helena in Sc 2 with the way Demetrius spoke to her in Sc 1. The language of Oberon and Puck is used to separate them from the world of mortals and also to give their speeches a chanting quality.

■ Self-test questions Act 2

Uncover the plot

Delete two of the three alternatives given, to find the correct plot. Beware possible misconceptions and muddles.

Puck (also called Phillida/Robin Goodfellow/Oberon) introduces – and we then see – the argument between Oberon and Ariadne/Hippolyta/Titania over a changeling boy/Indian king/Theseus, whom she keeps for the sake of his beauty/mother/value. Oberon asks Puck to find a milk-white/luscious/purple flower with the power of a love potion, which he intends to use on Titania/Lysander/Bottom. He witnesses Demetrius/Lysander/Theseus spurning Hermia/Hipployta/Helena. He bids Puck put flower juice in Demetrius'/Titania's/Lysander's eyes, while he will do the same to Demetrius/Titania/Lysander. Oberon seizes his chance while Titania dances/sings/sleeps, but Puck comes upon Hermia/Helena/Titania asleep near Lysander/Demetrius/Oberon and puts juice in Helena's/Lysander's/Hermia's eyes. Theseus/Oberon/ Demetrius finally escapes Helena, who wakes Lysander: he declares his love for Hermia/Helena/Titania. She thinks he is sincere/mad/mocking, and flees. Hermia/Titania/Bottom wakes alone and also flees.

Who? What? Why? How?

1   Who do we see waking up, of all the characters who sleep, and who is left sleeping at the end?
2   Who runs after whom in this Act?
3   What power is in the flower juice used by Puck and Oberon?
4   What time limit does Oberon put on Puck's journey, and how fast does Puck say he can move?
5   What mistake does Puck make and why?
6   Why do Hermia and Lysander sleep apart, and what alternative interpretations of this affect the plot?
7   Why have Titania and Oberon fallen out?
8   Why does the flower sought by Puck have its name and power?
9   How has Titania and Oberon's quarrel upset the world of nature?
10 How does Demetrius escape Helena?

Who said that?

1   Who says: 'Thou speakest aright:/I am that merry wanderer of the night'?
2   Who says: 'That very time I saw, but thou couldst not,/Flying between the cold moon and the earth/Cupid'?
3   Who says: 'The spring, the summer,/The chiding autumn, angry winter, change/Their wonted liveries'?
4   Who says: 'Neglect me, lose me; only give me leave, /Unworthy as I am, to follow you'?
5   Who says: 'So thou, my surfeit and my heresy/Of all be hated, but the most of me', and to whom?

Open quotes

Find the line – and complete the phrase or sentence.

1   'And this same progeny of evils comes...'
2   'They do square, that all their elves...'
3   'I know a bank...'
4   'When thou wak'st, it is thy dear...'
5   'The will of man is by his reason sway'd...'

Act 3 Scene 1

The workmen rehearse in the woods. Puck plays a prank on Bottom by giving him the head of an ass. The other workmen run away. Bottom sings a song to show he is not afraid. The noise wakens the sleeping Titania who sees Bottom and falls in love with him.

The workmen arrive and find a 'marvellous convenient place' for their rehearsal. Without realising it, they pick a spot near the sleeping Titania. They begin to discuss the play and it is obvious at once that they have no real idea of what a play is all about.

Bottom worries about killing himself. Snug apologises for being a lion

Bottom is worried that in their play his character, Pyramus, must draw a sword

and kill himself. He says this will never 'please', because it will upset the ladies in the audience and that, for the same reason, they cannot possibly have a lion on stage. Snug the joiner, who is to play the lion, agrees, as do all the others. It never occurs to any of them that the ladies at the court will have seen plays before and will know that the characters are not real, and their solution to these problems is more absurd than the 'problems' themselves.

The workmen

They decide there must be a piece at the start of the play (a prologue), to explain everything to the audience – that Bottom does not really kill himself and that the lion is not really a lion but is Snug, the joiner. Bottom says that

Snug's face must be seen through the lion's neck and he must speak to the audience to reassure them that he is not really a terrible lion. Their next headache involves getting moonlight into the play, because the script says that

Moon

Pyramus and Thisbe meet by moonlight. Quince says someone may have to represent or 'disfigure' (he means be the 'figure' of!) moonlight if there isn't a moon that night. The script also says that Pyramus and Thisbe speak to each other through a chink in a wall. Bottom suggests that someone must dress up in lumps of plaster, soil and stone and pretend to be a wall. They will have to hold their hands and fingers up to represent the chink.

Humour
The incongruity of 'hempen home-spuns' rehearsing a noble tragedy: note their absurdly literal-minded devices to deal with problems like the lion, moonshine and the wall.

More confusion between illusion and reality

The workmen fail to understand the difference between acting or pretending

Illusion

in a play (theatrical illusion) and reality. They think that they must have real moonlight. They worry that the audience will think that Snug is a real lion and that Pyramus really kills himself. Although this scene is written as farce, a serious point is also being made. The workmen are worried that their audience will confuse illusion with reality in the play. This is comic irony because that is exactly where the workmen themselves are confused. It connects this scene with the main action, because the lovers in the wood are also unable to tell illusion from reality. When Bottom has his head changed into

Love

that of an ass, he too enters a world of magic and illusion and will not be sure whether it was real or not. Titania cannot tell the difference between reality and illusion when the flower juice makes her fall in love with the ridiculous creature that Bottom has become.

The workmen's rehearsal degenerates into broad farce as they bungle their

Order

lines. Bottom begins to speak (as Pyramus) and mixes up 'odorous' flowers, meaning sweet smelling, with 'odious', meaning offensive and repugnant. Flute, who is playing Thisbe, gets his lines wrong, confuses stage directions and lines and pronounces 'Ninus' tomb' as 'Ninny's tomb'. Our amusement increases as the director Quince tries to keep his temper and as Bottom re-enters, transformed into a strange monster.

Bottom is made an ass of

Puck, who has been watching the rehearsal, has changed Bottom's head into

Puck

that of an ass for a prank. The other workmen, believing that the monster is real, run away in terror. Puck says he will chase them and change himself into a horse, a dog, a hog, a headless bear or a fire to frighten them even more. Snout returns and tells Bottom he is changed, Quince returns and says Bottom is 'translated' (he means 'transformed'!). Thinking they are trying to frighten him and are ridiculing him, Bottom accuses them of trying to 'make an ass of' him. Bottom now looks a fool and an 'ass'. (Note that in Shakespeare's day the word 'ass' would not have been used in the modern

Illusion

American sense to mean 'backside' but only to mean 'fool'.) The man who wanted to act all the parts in the play himself has now got a part he did not expect. His friends run away and Bottom decides to walk up and down singing to show them that they have not frightened him by their trick. This is ironic because it is they who have run off in terror of him. Bottom's singing awakens Titania.

'Reason and love keep little company together...'

The ultimate absurdity is reached when Titania awakens and instantly falls in

Titania

love with Bottom. Interestingly, the ass-headed Bottom now begins to talk a deal more sense than he ever did when he was himself. This is another example of dreams and illusion sometimes making more sense than reality in the play. An example of this occurs at once when Bottom says to Titania that 'reason and love keep little company together nowadays'. This is an ironic comment on Lysander's remark to Helena at the end of Act 2, when he told her that his 'reason' (logic) had now led him to love her. Often in Shakespeare's plays the clowns or fools seem wiser than their betters.

Order

In the same way Bottom says that Titania has 'little reason' (meaning not much reason) for thinking that she loves him. These words also have a clever double meaning, for the magic potion has deprived Titania of the power of 'reason'. This is emphasised in a clever comment when she says to Bottom 'thou art as wise as thou art beautiful'. She thinks Bottom is beautiful because of the magic potion and thinks whatever he says and does is wise and wonderful. Only the audience is in a position to appreciate the irony of this.

Bottom is carried away by fairies

Titania says she will give Bottom some fairies to look after him and fetch him

Nature

Moon

Love

jewels, whilst she sings to him as he sleeps on a bed of pressed flowers. The fairies are told to feed Bottom on apricots, blackberries ('dewberries'), grapes, figs and mulberries, to bring him honey stolen from bees and to 'pluck the wings from painted butterflies to fan the moonbeams from his sleeping eyes'. Bottom is introduced to his servants and jokes with them about their names.

The scene ends with another of its several references to the moon and its light. Titania says the moon looks sad ('looks with a watery eye') and makes all the flowers weep also, as if she is in sorrow for some 'enforced chastity'. Remember that the idea that it is sad for someone to have to remain forever 'chaste' (a virgin) was introduced by Theseus when he warned Hermia at the start of the play that she might have to become a nun (a 'barren sister') if she disobeyed her father. The scene ends with Bottom being led away by the fairies to Titania's bower.

Imagery, language and verse

The situation is farcical, with incongruous exchanges between Bottom and the fairies, but Titania's speeches (full of imagery of fruits, insects and the moon) dignify the scene.

Act 3 Scene 2

Puck tells a delighted Oberon about Titania's love for Bottom. Oberon realises Puck's mistake with the flower when he sees Demetrius and Hermia arguing. Oberon repeats the spell with Demetrius who then joins with Lysander in worshipping Helena. Confusion and violent arguments among the lovers lead Lysander and Demetrius to the brink of a duel. To put things right, Oberon orders Puck to keep them apart until finally, with them all asleep, the remedy can be applied to Lysander's eye.

Puck tells Oberon that Titania is now in love with 'a monster'. He summarises what has just happened and his speech contains some fine imagery. He describes the workmen rushing about in confusion and pictures their

31

Puck

bewilderment when they see Bottom with his ass's head as being like startled jackdaws and geese that, 'Rising and cawing at the gun's report, sever themselves, and madly sweep the sky'. Puck tells Oberon that he also put the flower juice into the eyes of the sleeping Athenian youth. Oberon is delighted, but they are about to discover Puck's error.

Demetrius and Hermia arrive

The lovers

Illusion

Demetrius is in love with Hermia but is desperate because Hermia does not return his love. She is upset that Lysander was not there when she woke up and she angrily suspects that Demetrius has killed him. She accuses him and leaves in fury. Demetrius, deciding not to follow her, lies down and goes to sleep. Oberon and Puck realise their mistake and Oberon tells Puck to go and find Helena and bring her to Demetrius . He then puts the flower juice on Demetrius' eyes. Puck returns with news that Helena is nearby with Lysander. Anticipating more amusement as both men will soon love Helena, Puck says 'Lord, what fools these mortals be!'

Lysander arrives with Helena

Lysander, under the influence of the magic potion, protests his love for Helena

Love

and his indifference to Hermia. He tells Helena 'I had no judgement when to her I swore'. Demetrius awakens, sees Helena, also falls in love with her and declares his love in the most exaggerated and ridiculous terms. Helena is convinced that both men are making fun of her. The anger of the lovers increases as the scene progresses. The fact that most of the confusion comes about because of comic mistakes only serves to increase the amusement of Puck and of the audience.

Hermia arrives and another quarrel breaks out

The arrival of Hermia signals the climax of this scene, which is the longest in

Order

the play. At first she is relieved to have found Lysander, but soon becomes bewildered by the behaviour of the other three. She is stunned when Lysander tells her that he now hates her. Helena suspects that Hermia is in the plot to humiliate her, and complains of the treacherous way her old friend is treating her. The two men join in the argument, each saying that he loves Helena more than the other, and each claiming to be the better person. They hurl abuse at each other and at Hermia and it looks as if a fight is about to develop. Although this may be entertaining, both characters are gripped by powerful emotions, the result of equally powerful illusions.

Meanwhile a spiteful and petty quarrel has broken out between the women. Each thinks that the other has stolen her lover. Hermia, who is not as tall as Helena, calls her a 'painted maypole' and says that, tall as she is, Hermia will still scratch her eyes out. Notice that the actions of the women are not caused by the magic potion, but are a reaction to the behaviour of the men. Lysander and Demetrius go off to fight a duel.

Characters

Detailed study of this scene is crucial to your essay. Can they really mean what they say: 'vile thing', 'loathed medicine', 'you canker-blossom', 'vixen', 'dwarf', etc?

Oberon decides that enough is enough

Oberon blames Puck for what has happened. He is determined to prevent

Oberon

the two men fighting each other. He tells Puck to bring darkness and fog so that the men will lose each other. Then he is to imitate each man's voice to the other, leading them about, until they are separated and exhausted. When they are both asleep, Puck is to put a potion into the eyes of Lysander as an antidote to the first potion, so that his normal vision is restored.

Oberon says that the lovers will then return to Athens. He will go to beg the Indian boy from Titania and release her from the power of the magic potion so that 'all things shall be peace'. Puck observes that dawn ('Aurora's harbinger') is coming and they must hurry, for 'ghosts wandering here and there troop home to churchyards'. Such 'damned spirits' must not be about at dawn but must forever be 'with black-brow'd night'. This was a traditional superstition. Oberon says they are not like that, they 'are spirits of another sort' and can walk the earth at dawn. In a lovely description of sunrise, he says he has often wandered the forests as the sun has begun to rise over the sea:

'Even till the eastern gate all fiery red
Opening on Neptune with fair blessed beams
Turns into yellow gold his salt green streams.'

Puck successfully exhausts both men as instructed and they sleep. Helena too falls asleep and Hermia follows.

'Cupid is a knavish lad thus to make poor females mad!'

Puck speaks this line as Hermia lies down to sleep. The amusement of this scene comes as much from the bewildered and exhausted state of the women

33

The lovers

Puck

as from the foolish behaviour of the men. Lysander and Demetrius think they are acting nobly, honourably and sensibly, whereas, in fact, they are being led a merry dance by Puck and the potion and appear to us as ridiculous figures of fun. The women are driven frantic by the strange behaviour of the men and are weary of the chase through the wood. Several different kinds of 'madness' are therefore illustrated at the end of this scene. The scene closes with a gentle song from Puck in which he says all will be well again when the lovers wake up: 'Jack shall have Jill, nought shall go ill; the man shall have his mare again, and all shall be well.'

Farce: the real and the artificial

Farce at its funniest requires a situation where characters, acting seriously, are nevertheless driven into absurd actions, whether through misunderstandings or misdemeanors. A farce generally moves through three stages: the creation of the crazy situation, the stage where the characters struggle to escape or make sense of it, and (usually, not always) the explanation or return to normality. In *A Midsummer Night's Dream* the farce of the lovers' plot is nearly all crammed into this one scene of multiple exits and entrances. The first effect of Puck's mistake is Hermia's fury at the disappearance of Lysander, and Oberon then makes things temporarily worse by administering the love-juice to Demetrius. By the end of the scene, the crazy world of farce has ended in sleep.

One of the most important elements in farce is that the characters take it seriously: it is no joke for them. Note here the fury of the arguments and, particularly, the convincing character responses. Helena's certainty that it's all a malicious scheme to mock her rings especially true.

> **Humour**
> Hermia's exit line, 'I am amazed, and know not what to say', sums up the problems of farce characters from Shakespeare to television sitcom.

Verse and rhyme

Shakespeare regularly uses blank verse for noble and serious speeches, prose for comic and informal speeches. In this play there is an unusual amount of rhyme which always sounds less natural than blank verse. In this scene the supernaturals use rhyme as usual, as do the lovers at first. Read through the lovers' arguments and find where the argument becomes too violent for the artificiality of rhyme. And what does Shakespeare choose for the sleep-and-calm final stages of the scene?

34

A world of contrasts

Contrasts are emphasised between disorder and harmony, love and hate, dreams and reality. The play shows how it is unwise to expect always to understand everything by logic and reason alone. The world of the imagination has its own kind of truth and makes its own kind of sense, just like the world of dreams. Even though Puck thinks mortals are fools, Oberon sees it as the responsibility of the fairy world to help them.

Notice that at the end of the untangling of the confusion with the potion, Oberon does not tell Puck to put the antidote in the eyes of Demetrius. Think back to when Lysander told Theseus that Demetrius used to love Helena. By leaving the flower juice in Demetrius' eyes, Oberon is putting things back the way they were. Demetrius will continue to love Helena and she, of course, has always loved him.

■ Self-test questions Act 3

Uncover the plot

Delete two of the three alternatives given, to find the correct plot. Beware possible misconceptions and muddles.

Puck reports to Oberon/Titania/Theseus on his pranks, including the fact that Titania loves Bottom/Lysander/Demetrius, who has been given an ass's/bear's/bull's head during the play rehearsal. Meanwhile Demetrius/Lysander/Bottom has caught up with Hermia, who still spurns him, desperate to find Demetrius/Lysander/Bottom. Oberon realises that Demetrius/Lysander/Hermia has not been charmed as planned; he now charms him, as Helena enters, pursued by the enchanted Lysander/Bottom/Hermia. Demetrius wakes and also declares love for Helena/Hermia/Titania. Hermia joins them, is distraught to find that Lysander/Demetrius/Helena hates her, and blames Helena/Demetrius/Puck. Meanwhile, Helena accuses all three of conspiring to bait/injure/love her. As the men are about to fight, Oberon/Theseus/Helena steps in: Puck separates/encourages/enchants them and, as all four lovers sleep, puts love juice/antidote juice/dew on Lysander's/Demetrius'/Hermia's eyes. With Oberon on his way to do the same for Titania/Helena/Bottom, all will be put right.

Who? What? Where? Why? How?

1 Who is the shorter and who the taller of the two girls: find a quote to prove it!
2 Who has flower juice left in his eyes at the end of all this – and why is it all right?
3 What four problems do the workmen foresee in their play?
4 What does Titania command her fairies to find for Bottom?
5 Where in the wood do the workmen find a 'marvellous convenient place' to rehearse?
6 Where, according to Puck, do ghosts go at night, and at dawn?
7 Why does Bottom start singing, and what does this do to move the plot along?

8   Why does Hermia 'chide' Demetrius, and why does shy say she should 'use' him 'worse'?

9   How does Oberon prevent violent conflict between Lysander and Demetrius?

10   How does Puck describe Bottom to Oberon?

Who said that?

1   Who says: 'The summer still doth tend upon my state'?

2   Who says: 'Reason and love keep little company nowadays', and why is this ironic?

3   Who says: 'And though she be but little, she is fierce!', of whom, and to what effect?

4   Who says: 'Shall we their fond pageant see? Lord, what fools these mortals be!'?

5   Who says: 'When they next wake, all this derision/Shall seem a dream and fruitless vision.'?

Open quotes

Find the line – and complete the phrase or sentence.

1   'I see their knavery...'

2   'Of thy misprision must perforce ensue...'

3   'You both are rivals, and love Hermia...'

4   'Even till the eastern gate...'

5   'Jack shall have Jill...'

Connections

There are several different 'worlds' and plot strands in the play: royals, lovers, workmen, fairies. They are all interconnected. Let's explore.

1   What three forms of 'illusion' link the workmen, lovers and fairies?

2   What do both Helena and Bottom think is going on when those around them behave strangely?

3   Who goes to sleep in this Act, and why?

4   Who wakes up in this Act, why, and with what consequences?

5   What connection is made by the following?
     'Pyramus and Thisbe meet by moonlight'.
     Bottom says Titania has 'little reason' to love him.
     Titania says the moon is 'lamenting some enforced chastity'.

Contrasts

This Act is full of the contrast between the human and fairy realms. The argument between the lovers and the effect of the potion also creates some lively changes of tune! Let's explore.

1   Find a rhyming couplet of Titania's that contrasts the world of fairies and humans.

2   How does nature, under fairy influence, treat Bottom? By contrast, how are the workmen and Hermia treated by nature without 'taming' by fairies?

3   The last thing Demetrius said to Helena (2,2) was simply: 'Stay on thy peril; I alone will go'. What is the first thing he says to her when he wakes enchanted?

4   Helena speaks of 'all school-days' friendship' with Hermia. What does she say about this later in the argument?

5   What two sorts of spirit are there, according to Puck and Oberon? What love image shows the difference between them?

Act 4 Scene 1

Titania and her fairies lead in Bottom and pamper him. They all sleep. Oberon now has the changeling boy so Titania is released from the spell. The ass's head is removed from Bottom. The mortals are left asleep as the fairies depart. Theseus arrives with Hippolyta and Egeus. The four lovers awaken and Theseus says they shall all be married along with himself and Hippolyta. After they have left, Bottom awakens and tries to remember his strange dream.

This scene opens with Titania still infatuated with Bottom. He still has the

head of an ass. Titania strokes his cheeks, puts roses on his brow and kisses his ears. Bottom asks very politely for something to eat: he fancies dry oats, sweet hay, or a handful or two of dried peas. When Titania asks him if he would like some music, he answers in all innocence that he would,

Titania

because he has 'a reasonable good ear' for music. The joke about his liking good music is carried further when he asks for a tune on 'the tongs and the bones', which were clappers of bone or wood that were held in one hand and rattled together. The idea that these could have produced beautiful music is also a joke. Titania sends her fairies away, puts her arms around Bottom and tells him she loves him, as they both go to sleep.

Humour

Bottom is an incongruous mix of Titania's lover (heavy-handed version of her insect imagery), an ass (jokes about oats, hay, etc.) and the familiar Bully Bottom.

The imagery of nature

The imagery of nature and natural things is raised to new heights here. Titania compares her embrace of Bottom to the way plants wind round each other:

'So doth the woodbine the sweet honeysuckle
Gently entwist; the female ivy so
Enrings the barky fingers of the elm.'

This image skilfully sums up an important idea in the play. Titania winds

her arms around Bottom. She is the beautiful 'female ivy' and Bottom is the rough and 'barky' elm. The ivy depends on the elm for support. The elm is made more beautiful by the ivy. They are wound together like honeysuckle and woodbine. She represents the mystery and beauty of the spirit world. He

Nature

represents the foolish, rough world of mortals. The beautiful and magical world of the imagination, dreams and night should support and be in harmony with the ordinary, logical world of daylight. These images of

37

support and harmony neatly explain the Elizabethans' view of the proper relationship between the mysterious world of nature and the everyday world of mankind.

Love

The audience will find this scene amusing because of the jokes and because it is ridiculous. The scene is also beautiful and touching because the characters are sincere and innocent.

The action moves from chaos towards harmony again

Until now, Puck has been used solely to cause confusion and mischief. Oberon

Order

now tells him that he wants to make amends to Titania, who has given him the changeling boy. He resolves to return Titania to normal and tells Puck to remove the ass's head from Bottom. When Bottom wakes up he will go back to Athens with the other mortals. Oberon says they will all think that what has happened to them has been only 'the fierce vexation

of a dream'. From now on, Puck and Oberon will use their power and magic to return everything to harmony.

The way music is used in the play

Oberon

Oberon puts the antidote into the eyes of Titania and when she wakes up she sees Bottom for what he is and says she loathes his ugliness. Oberon and Titania summon up music and begin to dance.

Notice how music, because of its use of harmony, often appears when other kinds of 'harmony' are being suggested, as between two lovers or within a society. Here the presence of music shows that the action of the play is moving away from discord and towards harmony.

Order

Theseus arrives. More about music

Theseus, Hippolyta, Egeus and their attendants arrive to the sound of horns and the baying of hunting dogs. This shatters the atmosphere created by the tender music and dancing of Oberon and Titania. Theseus says they 'have the vaward' of the day, meaning that they have the front-part (vanguard, or first place) in the day. He means that they have seen daybreak; that they are up with the dawn. Dreaming and illusions belong to the night and with the arrival of the day they have been scattered.

This moment marks the point when the action of the play leaves the mischief and magic of darkness and the fairy world and returns to the world of daylight and sanity. The music imagery is used to emphasise this, when Theseus says that Hippolyta will 'hear the music of my hounds' and that, as they run up the valley, they will hear 'the musical confusion of hounds and echo in

Illusion conjunction'. Although Theseus uses his hounds for hunting, he says that they are not very good at chasing things. He likes them mostly for the way their barking and baying produce a kind of harmony. This is what he means when he calls them 'match'd in mouth like bells'. Harmony is more important to Theseus than other qualities, however outstanding.

The lovers are discovered

The hunting party stumble across the four lovers, and Lysander begins to try to explain what has happened to them all. Egeus speaks for the last time in the play and asks Theseus to pass judgement upon Lysander for stealing away with his daughter. Demetrius interrupts to say that he now loves Helena. He does not want to marry Hermia any more. Theseus says this is good news

The lovers and he will override Egeus' wishes. Demetrius shall marry Helena. Lysander shall marry Hermia. Although Egeus has the law on his side, the play shows that Theseus is here being wiser than the law. Theseus' judgement is therefore a better kind of justice than the letter of the law.

More about the language in the play

Notice Demetrius' language here. As long as they were in the wood, the speech of Demetrius and Lysander was full of overstatement. The audience would understand that this showed a lack of real sincerity in their words and that this effect was being produced by the magic potion, so that the

Illusion 'real' characters were not actually speaking. The language here shows a complete absence of this exaggerated style of speech and suggests that the 'real' person is now speaking. The lovers seem to have had their 'false' feelings transformed by their experience in the wood.

Theseus and his hunting party leave and the lovers discuss their strange experiences. Demetrius observes that the events of the night seem diminished and obscured:

'These things seem small and undistinguishable,
Like far-off mountains turned into clouds.'

This image is very appropriate. Far-off mountains may be huge and solid

Order

things, but they are sometimes difficult to distinguish from clouds that are in reality made of mist and fog. The suggestion is that dreams and other irrational things – like love – are the other side or another aspect of the real, logical, common-sense world. It is sometimes impossible to tell what is real and solid and what is insubstantial and unreal. Notice how all four 'bewitched' characters – Lysander, Demetrius, Titania and Bottom – believe that they have simply dreamed their strange experiences. This is yet another 'illusion', an extra layer of unreality in the play.

Characters

The young men say more than the women, but all express only bemusement and present happiness. The return to normal is quickly accomplished – explanations might be dangerous!

Bottom's dream

Bottom wakes up after the others have left and speaks a short soliloquy. At

Illusion

first he thinks that the other workmen must be somewhere about but, when he realises they are not, he assumes that they have run off and left him asleep. He talks about his wonderful dream. His version of what happened is typical of the glorious muddle he makes of everything. He mixes up his words and talks about how 'the eye of man hath not heard, the ear of man hath not seen, man's hand is not able to taste, his tongue to conceive, nor his heart to report, what my dream was.' He thinks his dream should be written

Order

down by his friend Peter Quince. He says it would make a good ballad, which is a song that tells a story. The ballad should be called 'Bottom's Dream' because it has 'no bottom'. He means that his dream cannot be 'bottomed' or understood fully. This is another clever use of words. Dreams often fail to make any sense in reality, as the play has just shown, so they have no 'bottom'. Shakespeare's play also escapes attempts fully to understand it in 'reality'.

One scene – four plots

All four plots (stories) of the play, as described in the **Plot synopsis**, are here brought together in one scene and all either come to an end or have a forseeable ending. The quarrel between Oberon and Titania ends, as do the quarrels and confusions of the lovers. The two remaining stories will end at court. We now know three marriages will conclude the story begun in the opening lines of the play. Now that Bottom has returned to normal, he is ready to return to his fellow actors and perform at the celebrations.

Note that, although virtually all the characters appear in this scene, Shakespeare keeps the fairy and mortal royalty apart: Oberon and Titania leave, Theseus and Hippolyta then arrive. What happens in the final scene of the play which also includes both royal couples?

Five acts, nine scenes

This scene is typical of a play that, unusually for Shakespeare, has only one or two scenes in each act. Only three locations are used: five central scenes in the wood, framed by scenes at court and Quince's house at each end of the play. A whole variety of characters and plots overlap: in this scene work out what reasons bring together the Athenian court, four lovers and a weaver in a magic wood? Throughout the play characters act in a 'control' situation. They are in an enclosed setting and their actions are controlled by Theseus (first and last scenes) or Oberon (the scenes in the wood). The exceptions may be Act 1 Sc 2 and Act 4 Sc 2: does Peter Quince control the actions of his cast?

Act 4 Scene 2

Bottom arrives and he and the rest of the workmen depart for the Duke's palace.

This very short scene acts as a transition between the previous scene with the

lovers waking up, and the final scene in the play. It contains all the usual mix-ups that the audience have come to expect whenever the workmen appear. They are looking for Bottom and say that they cannot do the play without him. Quince calls Bottom 'a very paramour for a sweet voice'. Flute corrects him and says he means 'paragon', (a model of perfection), not 'paramour' (lover)! Starveling says that Bottom has been 'transported', meaning that they cannot find him because he has been mysteriously carried away. This is comic because lovers were said to be 'transported' by love, meaning their feelings were moved onto another, higher plane. Because the audience knows what has been happening to Bottom in the wood, they will understand Starveling's remark in a way he did not mean. When Bottom appears, he seems about to tell his friends where he has been and what has happened to him. With a delightful switch of direction he changes his mind and gives everybody instructions to prepare for their play, because he is sure they will be asked to perform for Theseus.

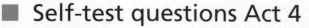

■ Self-test questions Act 4

Uncover the plot

Delete two of the three alternatives given, to find the correct plot. Beware possible misconceptions and muddles.

Titania and Bottom/Theseus/Puck settle close by the sleeping fairies/lovers/hounds. Oberon/Theseus/Puck has already met her and been given the bower/flower/child he wanted, and now wants peace. Puck/Cobweb/Oberon releases Titania, who, waking, loves/laughs at/loathes Bottom's face, while Puck/Cobweb/Oberon removes the ass's head. The five/six/four sleepers are charmed deeper, as the fairies dance and depart, resolving to disrupt/miss/bless the festivities in Athens the next day/the following midnight/the next full moon. Theseus and Hippolyta arrive to hunt with bulls/hounds/horses, and wake the lovers.Lysander/Demetrius/Hermia confesses the elopement plan, Theseus/Hippolyta/Egeus demands punishment, but Lysander/Demetrius/Egeus confesses his change of heart: Theseus rules that all shall be hanged/banished/married. Bottom/Titania/Helena wakes alone, and hurries to join the players.

Who? What? Where? Why? How?

1   Who are 'all these five' that Oberon orders to be put in a deeper sleep?
2   To whom does Egeus appeal, and who disappoints him?
3   What characteristics is Bottom aware of that the audience identify with his transformed shape?
4   What does Bottom cry as he awakes?
5   Where do Titania and Bottom come to sleep?
6   Where is Scene 2 set, and what change has come over the language and mood?
7   Why does Oberon now want to release Titania from the spell?
8   Why does Theseus like his hounds so much?
9   How do the workmen greet Bottom's return, and why?
10 How does Demetrius describe his change of feeling towards Helena?

Who said that?

1   Who says: 'Are you sure that we are awake?'
2   Who says: 'I beg the law, the law upon his head', and of whom?
3   Who says: 'The eye of man hath not heard, the ear of man hath not seen... what my dream was.'?
4   Who says: 'We the globe can compass soon/Swifter than the wand'ring moon'?
5   Who says: 'He is a very paramour for a sweet voice!', of whom, and why is this funny?

Open quotes

Find the line – and complete the phrase or sentence.
1   'So doth the woodbine...'
2   'How comes this gentle concord in the world...'
3   'For she his hairy temples...'
4   'These things seem small...'
5   'For we are to utter sweet breath; and I doubt not...'

Connections

There are several different 'worlds' and plot strands in the play: royals, lovers, workmen, fairies. They are all interconnected. Let's explore.
1   Find a six-line passage where all four story strands begin to connect.
2   What two story strands are reintroduced into the action, having been mainly forgotten in the wood?

3   What 'dreams' feature in this Act?
4   What 'music' features in this Act?

Called to order
1   What is magic used for in this Act?
2   Who and what arrive as the fairies depart, and to what effect?
3   What do you notice about how the fairies address each other after Titania awakens?
4   What do you notice about the descriptions of the hounds' calls? How might this back up the move back to order and harmony?
5   How does Theseus' parting couplet finally establish the new mood of order?

Act 5 Scene 1

Theseus has been told about the experiences of the lovers in the wood. He thinks that love has caused them to imagine it all. Hippolyta is not so sure. The workmen's play is performed. Oberon blesses the marriages of the human lovers.

Theseus and Hippolyta are discussing the stories that the four lovers have told them about their time in the wood. Theseus feels that their accounts are 'more strange than true'. He thinks they have been imagining things. He says they are like poets whose powerful imaginations sometimes make them live on the edge of insanity:

The lovers

> 'The lunatic, the lover and the poet
> Are of imagination all compact.'

Moon

His use of the word 'lunatic' is interesting because it comes from 'luna', meaning the moon. Theseus is saying that too much imagination or too much passion gives people a distorted view of the world and that people who are in love sometimes imagine things are there when they are not. They can imagine someone is very beautiful (have 'Helen's beauty') when really they look like a gypsy (have 'a brow of Egypt'). A dark complexion, especially a Moorish or African one, was considered ugly by the Elizabethans. Theseus says the poet is similar. Poets can create things out of their imaginations, out of nothing:

Love

> 'The poet's eye, in a fine frenzy rolling,
> Doth glance from heaven to earth, from earth to heaven;
> And as imagination bodies forth
> The forms of things unknown, the poet's pen
> Turns them to shapes, and gives to airy nothing
> A local habitation and a name.'

This is Theseus's explanation for what has happened to the lovers. It is also a good summary of what Shakespeare has done in *A Midsummer Night's Dream*.

Theseus says they will see the workmen's play

Theseus reads through the list of entertainment on offer for the three hours

Illusion

between their after-supper meal and bed-time. He comes to the workmen's description of their play: 'A tedious brief scene of young Pyramus and his love Thisbe, very tragical mirth'. Theseus is amused that something could be merry and tragic at the same time; be brief and yet still be tedious. He says this is like having hot ice. The audience finds this amusing, because

by now they know only too well how the workmen's play can be tedious to watch, however short it is, and how it can be funny, even though it is supposed to be serious.

The workmen

Theseus' servant Philostrate, (Master of the Revels) gives an amusing account of the workmen's play. He says he has seen it and, although it is only a few words long, it is too long by that number of words. He says the play is 'tedious' because it is so hopelessly bad. He adds that the play is supposed to be a tragedy, because the character Pyramus kills himself, but that

it is acted in such a ham-fisted way that he laughed until he cried when he saw it. He advises them not to watch it because it is so poor. Theseus decides that they will see the play. He says that the workmen have done the play out of a sense of service and duty to him and 'never anything can be amiss when simpleness and duty tender it'.

Order

Theseus knows that the workmen are not professional actors and their performance may be poor, but he values their other qualities more highly. You should remember that he felt the same way about his hunting hounds. Like the audience who have watched *A Midsummer Night's Dream*, Theseus has found that the most valuable parts of things may not be those that immediately meet the eye.

Another probable compliment to Queen Elizabeth I

Queen Elizabeth I often toured the country and, wherever she went, people put on entertainment for her. It is said that she always accepted these very graciously, no matter how amateurish and clumsy they were. It is likely that Theseus' attitude towards the workmen's play was therefore intended as another compliment by Shakespeare to the Queen.

Humour

Another variation on the clownish humour of the mechanicals: Peter Quince's mispunctuated Prologue. To appreciate the skill of the humour, you need to work out what he intends to say.

Quince speaks the play's prologue

Quince begins the workmen's play with the prologue. He gets his speech muddled and ends up saying the opposite of what he intended. He says 'All

for your delight, we are not here' and joins parts of two separate sentences together. He means to say that their intention is to delight their audience and that the workmen are not there to upset people. The courtiers find this hilarious and begin making unkind comments which continue throughout the workmen's play. You should notice that

The workmen

Quince's speech could have made sense, but didn't because of the way he presented it. What he did say made sense, if you looked at it differently. This is the theme of reality and appearance, sense and nonsense, again. Theseus says the speech is 'like a tangled chain; nothing impaired, but all disordered.'

The workmen's play begins and is full of lines and phrases that are amusing, clumsy and ridiculous. Quince tries to use alliteration to stress his meaning but does it so badly that the effect is absurd – for example, his description of

Pyramus' death: 'with bloody, blameful blade he bravely broached his boiling bloody breast'. He does the same thing again when he says 'his dagger drew and died'. Much of the humour in the workmen's play comes from the deadly seriousness with which they perform it, and none more so than

The workmen

Bottom. The audience will find this scene amusing but in a

Order

different way from the courtiers. The courtiers mock the rough-handed workmen and their incompetent acting. The audience do not see an anonymous collection of workmen because they have got to know them. What they see are Bottom and Quince, Snout, Flute and Snug. By now they will have become quite fond of these bumbling but kind-hearted characters. The audience can laugh at the amateurish performance while also enjoying the wisecracks of the courtiers, but their amusement will be more affectionate.

The performance is full of clever references to the rest of *A Midsummer Night's Dream*. Notice how Demetrius is laughing at Quince's prologue and, when Theseus wonders whether the lion is going to speak, says: 'One lion may when many asses do'. This is an echo of what happened to Bottom.

Humour

A scene full of humorous contrast; e.g. the visual humour of the Moon followed by witticisms: 'the man should be put into the lantern', 'would he would change', etc.

'This is the silliest stuff that ever I heard'

Hippolyta, who makes this comment, finds the workmen's performances so awful that she cannot believe in the characters. Theseus reminds her that the audience must use their imagination to compensate for any lack of polish. He says that even the best actors are 'but shadows' and rely on the help of the audience to make the play believable. This is the thing that the workmen have not realised. By stepping outside their characters to talk directly to the audience, they are destroying the illusion they are trying to create. *A Midsummer Night's Dream* stresses the importance of imagination in the way everybody sees and understands the world. Imagination helps people to decide what is real and meaningful to them, in the emotional sense. All emotions, like love and hatred, are 'real' to the people experiencing them, but none of them can be seen, touched or tasted. To rely only on things that can be explained by logic and reason is to be blind to many important things that make people what they are.

Illusion

'Pyramus dies and dies and dies again'

The over-the-top death speech by Bottom starts with: 'O wherefore, Nature, didst thou lions frame…'. This is one of the most ludicrous parts of the workmen's play. Bottom tangles up the ending and says 'tongue, lose thy light; moon, take thy flight' but takes it all so seriously that the effect is comic. His speech ends with a hopelessly exaggerated death: 'Now die, die, die, die, die.' There is, however, something much more subtle going on here. The play of Pyramus and Thisbe described a situation that the lovers could actually have found themselves in if things had gone badly when Lysander and Demetrius were going to fight a duel.

The workmen

Illusion

Bottom and his friends fail to understand how drama works. They get mixed up between the world of illusion which they are trying to create in their play and the real world outside it. As the audience is actually watching Pyramus and Thisbe being performed inside *A Midsummer Night's Dream*, this is doubly clever. The audience is watching a play within a play. The confusion the workmen create by continually stepping outside their play to talk directly to their audience is no more ridiculous than the confusion the lovers became entangled in when they were in the wood. It is therefore ironic that the lovers sneer when they are watching the workmen's play. The lovers now see themselves as sophisticated courtiers and scoff at the workmen's efforts, which they think foolish. It is not so long since they themselves were behaving just as foolishly.

Thisbe finds the dead body of Pyramus

Order

Flute, who is playing Thisbe, begins a speech over the dead body of Pyramus. The humour comes from the language. Thisbe is supposed to be speaking delicate and moving love poetry, but this is made absurd by the words the workmen have chosen to use:

> 'These lily lips,
> This cherry nose,
> These yellow cowslip cheeks,
> Are gone, are gone!
> Lovers, make moan;
> His eyes were green as leeks.'

The effect is to shatter completely any dramatic effect that this doggerel might possibly have created. At the end of the play the 'dead' Bottom leaps up to interrupt a conversation between Demetrius and Theseus, which has the same effect.

No more, please!

Theseus politely refuses the offer of an epilogue and the audience can see that the courtiers have had more than enough. Theseus asks them to dance instead, after which the workmen leave. There is a neat parallel here. The last piece of dancing in the play was at the end of a piece of make-believe – when Titania and Oberon danced after the lovers had come out of the wood. On both occasions dancing is used to suggest or create a mood of harmony and peace.

'The iron tongue of midnight hath told twelve'

Order

Theseus announces that the bells have rung for midnight. This speech of his marks the last appearance of the human characters in the play. Notice how the mood at the end of the play is very different from that at the start. The play began with argument and disharmony and ends with agreement, happiness, laughter, dancing and harmony. All has now turned out well.

Marriage and harmony

Throughout the play, marriage has been shown as the proper ending for mature love. Women who are forced to endure a virgin's life are described as unfulfilled, lonely and barren. Any breakdown in the relationship between two lovers is seen as unnatural and likely to lead to trouble. Shakespeare's play emphasises the importance of harmony.

Puck appears

Puck

Now that the human characters have gone for the last time, Puck appears to say that it is the time of the spirit world again. He says that the spirit world is a world showing kindness towards mortals. The happiness of mortals is the fairies' main concern. The fairy world has come to the palace of Theseus to guard it. Notice how the speech of Puck, Oberon and Titania is in rhyming couplets. This chanting rhythm suggests a spell. The fairies scatter throughout the house to give magical protection to the mortals. The world of 'glimmering' moonlight has returned.

Imagery, language and verse

The play ends at the return of night and of the spirits. Love and harmony prevail, but the world of fear and violence is still there – look at Puck's first 12 lines.

Puck's final speech

Moon

Illusion

Puck says that if 'we shadows' have offended anyone, they should now feel happy that everything has come out all right in the end. Puck steps forwards to talk directly to the audience and to remind them that the play is only make-believe. This is very like what the workmen did in their play. This is another echo or reflection in the structure of Shakespeare's play.

The play is about dreams and reality, about the rational and the irrational and about how it is sometimes very hard to tell one from the other. Characters in the play are continually hiding from each other. Much of the play is to do with people finding out who they really love and who they really are. Characters sometimes appear to be what they are not, like Bottom, or the lovers. Some characters are not visible (not real) to others, like the fairies. Some characters are deliberately pretending to be other people, like the workmen in their play. Many characters have their understanding of reality distorted by their feelings or by magic. Puck's comment that the play is full of 'shadows' would fit all of these.

Theseus's hunting horns and baying hounds awoke the lovers from their sleep and from the world of illusions and dreams. Puck asks the audience for their applause – 'give me your hands, if we be friends' – and this noise will also signal the release of the audience from the magic spell that Shakespeare has woven in *A Midsummer Night's Dream* and bring to an end their brief stay in a world of imagination and illusion.

Happiness and harmony

The end of the play brings all the different stories together in a happy and harmonious way. The play began with arguments and discord and it ends in happiness and harmony. The frightening dreams of the wood are put down to overheated imaginations. The workmen's play is performed to much amusement, although Theseus clearly regards it as sincere and therefore honourable. The lovers are married along with Theseus and Hippolyta and the fairies arrive to bless the marriages. The audience have been reassured that all is well and have been asked by Puck to show their friendship and appreciation by their applause.

■ Self-test questions Act 5

Uncover the plot

Delete two of the three alternatives given, to find the correct plot. Beware possible misconceptions and muddles.

Theseus/Hippolyta/Philostrate thinks the lovers' story a dream/fantasy/lie, but Theseus/Hippolyta/Philostrate is not so sure. The couples meet after/before/during supper and are offered a list of two/three/four entertainments. Despite Demetrius'/Hipployta's/Philostrate's warnings, Theseus chooses Pyramus and Thisbe, because it is well-written/sincerely offered/well-rehearsed. Quince/Bottom/Snout delivers a garbled Prologue, and the play proceeds with wry commentary by Theseus and Helena/Demetrius/Philostrate. Thisbe's body/mantle/lantern is mauled by the lion; Pyramus, finding it, stabs himself, and Thisbe (played by Bottom/Snout/Flute), discovering him dead, does likewise. After a final epilogue/bergomask/song, the players depart and the others retire. The fairies come to bless/curse/visit the place, and the last word is left to Titania/Oberon/Puck.

Who? What? Where? Why? How?

1   Who is Philostrate?
2   Who is a Prologue, and who is an Epilogue in this Scene?
3   What separates Pyramus and Thisbe?
4   What do the Prologue and Puck's epilogue have in common?
5   Where does Theseus say 'the man should be put', and why, and why is this not possible?
6   Where do the fairies go?
7   Why does Hippolyta think there may be something to the lovers' story?
8   Why did Philostrate cry when he saw the play in rehearsal?
9   How have the workmen described their entertainment on the list?
10 How does Philostrate describe the players to Theseus?

Who said that?

1   Who says: 'I never may believe/these antique fables, nor these fairy toys', and why is this ironic?
2   Who says: 'Never anything can be amiss when simpleness and duty tender it'?
3   Who says: 'This is the silliest thing that ever I heard'?

4   Who says: 'No, I assure you, the wall is down that parted their fathers', and why is this ridiculous?
5   Who says: 'Give me your hands, if we be friends', and what does it mean?

Open quotes

Find the line – and complete the phrase or sentence.
1   'The lunatic, the lover...'
2   'Whereat with blade, with bloody...'
3   'Lovers to bed:...'
4   'And each several chamber bless...'
5   'If we shadows have offended...'

Connections

There are several different 'worlds' and plot strands in the play: royals, lovers, workmen, fairies. What connections are made by the following?
1   Thisbe is attacked by a lion.
2   Theseus says of Bottom/Pyramus: 'he might... yet prove an ass'.
3   Pyramus and Thisbe kill themselves for love.
4   The workmen dance before they depart.
5   Theseus refuses an epilogue from the players.
6   The moonlight glimmers in the palace.

General questions on the play

1   Of the four lovers, who loved whom before the action of the play started? Who loves whom as the play starts? Who loves whom when the enchantments are at their height? Who loves whom finally?
2   Using the mnemonic LOW MINDS (perhaps an apt phrase for the workmen), list some of the themes of the play that begin with each letter.

How to write a coursework essay

Most of you will use your study of *A Midsummer Night's Dream* to write a coursework essay fulfilling the Shakespeare requirement for GCSE English/English Literature. In writing this essay, you must meet certain requirements. In particular, you must show awareness (though not necessarily at great length) of social and historical influences, cultural contexts and literary traditions. You might consider such things as social class, the ready acceptance of the supernatural, or the use and distortion of Greek myth. It is also essential that you show considerable evidence of textual knowledge, even if the essay has a strong creative element. Types of response might include:

- scene analysis;
- character study;
- analysis of imagery and other linguistic features;
- dramatic effect of the play or one or more scenes;
- empathic response to character;
- reflections on a production.

If you are writing an analytical essay, the *most important* consideration is that you must develop an argument or explain a point of view consistently throughout. There is little to be gained by saying what Oberon does. What is important is that you relate his actions or words to your theme: the jealous rivalry between Oberon and Titania, the part played by magic and illusion, the development of farcical situations, or whatever you are writing about. Careful advance preparation will aid you in organising your theme or argument: making notes on the material, putting those notes in order, then working through two or three drafts of the essay. By doing this you can reach a decision on what each paragraph is to be about, as far as possible signalling this to the reader in the opening sentence, often called a *topic sentence* because it introduces the topic of the paragraph.

If you choose an imaginative/creative essay, the *first essential* is to reveal throughout your factual knowledge of the text and a soundly based interpretation of it. Mere imagination will not gain credit in textual study for GCSE English Literature.

The length of your essay will depend on the type of essay you write, your own wishes and your teacher's advice, but do bear in mind that it is only one of several pieces of coursework: there is no need for a 5000 word blockbuster.

Humour

A Midsummer Night's Dream is a comedy, one that consistently amuses and entertains in a variety of styles, though there is much in the play that is more magical than comical. A challenging title for your coursework essay, but one with plenty of opportunities to excel, would be:

> *Analyse the varieties of humour within* A Midsummer Night's Dream *and consider how effectively Shakespeare combines different types of humour. How far does the play's success depend on elements other than comedy?*

The order in which you consider the various elements is up to you, but your first task is to recognise what you are *not* asked to do: tell the story of some funny scenes or characters. Analysis, not narration, is required.

As a general term the comedy of **incongruity** can be applied to much of *A Midsummer Night's Dream*; this means that things simply don't fit together. What could be more incongruous than a workman with an ass's head being attended by a band of fairies? Or Athenian nobles scrambling through a wood in pursuit of an invisible voice?

The main element in the comedy is **farce**. Aimed purely to amuse, farce depends on misunderstandings taken seriously and on hopeless attempts to maintain dignity: you will see plenty of it in television sit-coms. It often leads to physical humiliation (whether it's trousers falling down or having to wear an ass's head). Farce in *A Midsummer Night's Dream* is targeted at all those who venture into the wood and you will notice how earnestly they all, lovers and mechanicals alike, take their predicaments. Are the misunderstandings confined to the victims? There is also farce in the ludicrous misunderstandings of *Pyramus and Thisbe*, but you may find a term like **low character comedy** or **buffoonery** better sums up most of the mechanicals' scenes.

Other forms of comedy to look for include the **malicious sport** of Oberon and Puck, and many varieties of **verbal comedy**. A *malapropism* is using the wrong word, often similar in sound to the correct word; where do we find this? Where do we find amusing use of insults, and use of **parody** mocking literary styles (some extreme versions of alliteration, for instance)? Oddly enough, the people who are trying hardest to be funny (the nobles in Act 5) are not very amusing.

The different types of comedy are blended together in many ways. Two examples will show how the various elements depend on each other. The malicious sport of the spirits becomes entangled in the world of mortals and creates situations from which farce can spring. Or, in the last scene, the farcical dramatic parody of *Pyramus and Thisbe* and the courtly wit of the audience depend on each other for effect.

Finally, what else is there apart from comedy? Romance, magic and a progress towards harmony are other main elements. Yet again you should be able to show that they relate to the comedy and how each affects the other. After all, to simplify, you could say that the main story-line uses magic to create comedy to satisfy romance and build a world of harmony.

Imagery, language and verse

The style in which *A Midsummer Night's Dream* is written is a key element in its effect. There is scope for any number of different approaches to this topic and there is space here to do no more than hint at them.

An examination of the uses of verse and prose could be rewarding. Apart from Shakespeare's normal division into verse for noble speech, prose for comedy and more casual speech, there are many other devices here. Where does he use rhyming couplets, and why? What use does he make of stanza patterns (Hermia and Helena at the end of Act 3 Sc 2, for instance)? What are the differences between the verse of the fairies, the court and the play-within-a-play?

Much of the imagery (of the Moon or Nature, for instance) is considered in the **Text commentary** and an essay on the imagery of the play would certainly be suitable. However, I have chosen to look at a title which forces you to have an opinion:

> *How does Shakespeare's use of language, verse and imagery help to create the sense of a world of illusion?*

Your first task is to define the world of illusion you are writing about. It is the magic world of fairies, but you will have noticed that Shakespeare's fairies are not like those in a fairy story: most are male, and they show more passion and malice than you might expect. The play presents the 'internal' world of the fairy kingdom, but also two forms of magic relative to humans: the tricks played on wanderers in the wood and the protection of the house of Theseus.

The main section of your essay should be about the features of style which emphasise the exotic other-worldliness of the fairies: the songs with their references to strangely described plants, birds and insects; the varying verse patterns, often short lines, like spells; the exotic imagery. An intensive examination of Act 2 Sc 1, would be of great assistance. Puck ('Hobgoblin') is placed firmly in an English tradition, with coarsely expressed images of tricks on 'gossips'. Oberon and Titania introduce a world of Classical myth, with Ariadne and Antiopa. Images of 'flying between the cold moon and the earth' or putting 'a girdle round about the earth in forty minutes' convince us that this is not our normal world and we accept their world of illusion.

However, you also need to look at how the language or verse of the human characters changes when they are absorbed into the world of illusion. It is important that you should note that the lovers, spell-bound, often speak as though in a trance, sometimes with artificial rhyming patterns. And what about the imagery used by Bottom in Titania's 'flowery bed'?

Characters

Character analysis is always a suitable topic for a coursework essay on a play or novel, but in *A Midsummer Night's Dream* it would be difficult to build an essay on one character. The best approach would be to examine the general characteristics of a group of characters and then analyse the differences within the group. You might choose the mechanicals or the two royal couples, but we will consider the young lovers.

> *What characteristics are shared by the young lovers in* A Midsummer Night's Dream? *How successfully does Shakespeare distinguish them from each other?*

This essay is best approached in the order of the question. Throughout the central section of the play the lovers can be seen very much as a unit. They are passionate, confused, easily roused to temper: the most violent quarrels, interestingly enough, are between the two women and between the two men, not between lovers and spurned lovers. You will find that they are all changeable in mood, the men being changeable in affection, but in the circumstances (love-juice, etc.) is this a real comment on their characters?

Having considered the 'wood' scenes in general (with copious textual evidence, of course), you need to examine the characters when they are 'themselves'. In Act 1 Sc 1, we can form certain judgements. What class are they? We are not told, but Egeus seems a trusted counsellor of the Duke and the young people have the confidence to speak frankly before Theseus. How old are they? Young, but old enough for Demetrius already to have 'made love to' Helena (courted her). Demetrius speaks only two lines (calling Lysander's proposal 'crazed') and is next seen being hateful to the loving and helpful Helena. Lysander, equally rude to Demetrius, shows a loving courage in his scene with Hermia. Her love appears equally bold and genuine. The most interesting character in the opening is Helena whose motivation in telling Demetrius of the flight is complex and who seems to seek suffering and self-pity from her opening line: 'Call you me fair?'. How far can you find these characteristics carried through into the scenes in the wood? You should find plentiful evidence for Helena, rather less, but sufficient, for the others.

It is also worth looking through Act 5 when all, again, is normal. Read all the speeches by the lovers. You may be disappointed at how little of their characters is revealed, but you need to express this in your essay.

The lovers would be a good choice for what is called an 'empathic' response; that is, a response to the play in the role of one of the characters. Helena's response to her initial betrayal by Demetrius, the adventures in the wood and the unlikely happy ending, could offer a moving and amusing re-telling of some of the events of the play.

Other topics

You could choose many more excellent topics than there is room to consider here, but we will briefly consider two of the syllabus suggestions:

Scene analysis: The first task is the choice of scene. Act 3 Sc 2, Act 4 Sc 1 and Act 5 Sc 1 would all be ideal. The second task is to analyse the scene, not simply record its events. In each of these there is enormous variety, revealing the contrasts in comedy, character and class that we have already considered in connection with other essays. Apart from these, and analysis of imagery and language, you should try to write about the scene as drama: how could you stage it, how would it work in performance?

Reflections on a production: If you have seen a production (better still, two, possibly one in the theatre and one on television), you can write about the play on stage. It is essential that you move beyond stating that Oberon was good and Bottom was funny and reflect on how the production confirmed/improved/clashed with your understanding of the play. How did the production distinguish the three different societies (fairies, nobles, workmen) in setting, costume and manner? Especially, what was the director's concept of the fairies? How did the magic and humour work? Was there any doubling, and why? What is suggested by doubling Theseus and Hippolyta with Oberon and Titania or even, as Northern Broadsides' recent production did to great effect, the mechanicals (excluding Bottom and Quince) with the fairies?

How to write an examination essay

Most of you will study *A Midsummer Night's Dream* as a coursework text, but it is useful to consider the approach to an examination essay on the play. The advice given below will be useful in helping you to approach any English Literature examination essays.

Before you start writing

- The first essential is thorough revision. It is important that you realise that even Open Book examinations require close textual knowledge. You will have time to look up quotations and references, *but only if you know where to look.*

- Read the questions very carefully, both to choose the best one and to take note of *exactly what you are asked to do.* Questions on *A Midsummer Night's Dream* are likely to be on subjects similar to those considered in **How to write a coursework essay**, but you must make sure you know what is being asked: an astonishing number of candidates answer the question they *imagine or hope* has been asked. For instance, discussing Oberon's relationship with Titania when the question asks about his effect on the mortals gains no credit. The most common error of all is to narrate a section of the play when a quite different question has been asked.

- Identify all the key words in the question that mention characters, events and themes, and instructions as to what to do: e.g. compare, contrast, comment, give an account, etc. Write a short list of the things you have to do.

- Look at each of the points you have identified and jot down what you are going to say about each.

- Decide in what order you are going to deal with the question's main points. Number them in sequence.

Writing the essay

- Try to summarise your response to the question so the examiner has some idea of how you plan to approach it. For instance, if you are writing about the types of humour in *A Midsummer Night's Dream*, you might start, 'At the centre of *A Midsummer Night's Dream* lies the farcical confusion brought about by Oberon and Puck, but the variety of humour in the play includes physical and verbal comedy, buffoonery and aristocratic wit.' *Do not* start, 'The first really funny scene is where the workmen get together to put on a play.' Jump straight into the essay, do not nibble at its extremities for a page and a half. A personal response will be rewarded, but you must always answer the question: as you write the essay *refer back to your list of points.*

- Answer *all the question.* Many students spend all their time answering just one part of a question and ignoring the rest. This prevents you gaining marks for the parts left out. If you look at the questions on **Humour** and **Characters** in **How to write a coursework essay**, you will see that the second sentence sets a new task: make sure you notice if examination questions do that. Similarly, failing to answer enough questions on the examination is a waste of marks which can always be gained most easily at the start of an answer.

- There is no 'correct' length for an essay. What you must do is spend the full time usefully in answering all parts of the question (spending longer than the allocated time by more than a few minutes is dangerous). Some people write faster than others: they don't always get the best marks!

- Use quotation or paraphrase when it is relevant and contributes to the quality and clarity of your answer. Extended quotations are usually unhelpful, and padding is a waste of time.

Self-test answers Act 1

Uncover the plot

Theseus and Hippolyta look forward to their wedding at the new moon Egeus complains that his daughter Hermia refuses to marry Demetrius, because she is in love with Lysander. (Demetrius was previously in love with Helena.) If disobedient, Hermia must choose death or life as a nun. The lovers complain that 'true lovers have been ever cross'd' and decide to escape to a house seven leagues from Athens. Helena wishes she was like Hermia: Hermia assures her she does not want Demetrius' love – indeed, she is escaping. Helena resolves to tell Demetrius of their plan. Meanwhile, under the direction of Quince, the workmen prepare a play: Bottom is to play Pyramus, with Flute as Thisbe.

Who? What? Where? Why? How?

1   Theseus, Duke of Athens and Hippolyta, Queen of the Amazons 1,1
2   Snug the joiner; Bottom 1,2
3   He is as nobly born and rich as Demetrius. He and Hermia are in love. Demetrius has courted Helena 1,1
4   Unrhymed verse (iambic pentameter), for 'ordinary' cultured speech. Changes to rhymed couplets after Hermia agrees to meet Lysander in the wood: established mood of lovers' declarations, and is associated with the less real world of the wood. Changes to prose for the workmen: establishes the 'class' difference
5   Lysander's rich aunt, a childless widow, outside the city 1,1
6   Athens
7   To win his gratitude (she hopes) and attention 1,1
8   He says he will roar mightily: they are afraid he will frighten the court ladies and get them hung 1,2
9   With poetry, love-tokens, moonlit serenades, locks of hair, rings, nosegays, sweetmeats etc. 1,1
10 He defeated her in battle 1,1

Who said that?

1   Egeus, of Hermia 1,1
2   Theseus 1,1
3   Helena 1,1
4   Lysander, of love 1,1
5   Bottom 1,2

Open quotes

1   'Hippolyta, I woo'd thee with my sword/And won thy love doing thee injuries.' 1,1
2   'And she, sweet lady, dotes,/Devoutly dotes, dotes in idolatry,/Upon this spotted and inconstant man.' 1,1
3   'Ay me! for aught that I could ever read,/Could ever hear by tale or history,/The course of true love never did run smooth.' 1,1
4   'The more I hate, the more he follows me .' (Hermia) 'The more I love, the more he hateth me.' (Helena) 1,1
5   'Love looks not with the eyes but with the mind;/And therefore is wing'd Cupid painted blind.' 1,1

Connections

1 Mischievous 'spirits' – the fairies – will awake in the wood and play pranks on them all
   'Bright things' – in the shape of the lovers – will indeed 'come to confusion' in the fairy's realm
   Hermia and friends will indeed find 'stranger companies' in the wood: the fairies 1,1
2 Lysander and Hermia 1,1 – and the workmen 1,2
3 At Theseus and Hippolyta's wedding (also to be the lovers' wedding, blessed by the fairies – connecting all four strands) 1,2

Lunacy

1 As a measure and seeming controller of time: 'Four happy days bring in/Another moon; but, O, methinks, how slow/The old moon wanes.' 1,1
2 As a 'silver bow/New-bent in heaven': apt because she is an Amazon, a warrior 1,1
3 Lysander. Hermia, if she chooses to become a nun 1,1
4 Phoebe beholding 'her silver visage in the wat'ry glass' (mirror) 1,1
5 Moonlight 1,2

■ Self-test answers Act 2

Uncover the plot

Puck (also called Robin Goodfellow) introduces – and we then see – the argument between Oberon and Titania over a changeling boy, whom she keeps for the sake of his mother. Oberon asks Puck to find a purple flower with the power of a love potion, which he intends to use on Titania. He witnesses Demetrius spurning Helena. He bids Puck put flower juice in Demetrius' eyes, while he will do the same to Titania. Oberon seizes his chance while Titania sleeps, but Puck comes upon Hermia asleep near Lysander and puts juice in Lysander's eyes. Demetrius finally escapes Helena, who wakes Lysander: he declares his love for Helena. She thinks he is mocking, and flees. Hermia wakes alone and also flees.

Who? What? Why? How?

1 Lysander – to fall in love with Helena. Hermia – alone and frightened. Titania sleeps on 2,2
2 Helena runs after Demetrius. Lysander runs after Helena 2,1 2,2
3 Poured in the eyes, it makes the person fall in love with the first living thing he or she sees 2,1
4 'Ere the Leviathan can swim a league'. Puck says he can go round the world in forty minutes 2,1
5 He 'juices' Lysander instead of Demetrius: he is the only Athenian youth he finds 2,2
6 Out of modesty. Puck thinks it fear, so Lysander must be the disdainful youth he seeks: he 'juices' him by mistake. Helena thinks Lysander is dead or hurt, so wakes him to fall in love with her 2,2
7 Because Titania will not give Oberon the changeling child to be his servant 2,1
8 Cupid's arrow struck it: it is full of love without object – idle, hence 'Love-in-idleness' 2,1

9 There are fogs, overflowing rivers ruining crops, moonlight creating rheumatic diseases, early frost and seasons confused 2,1

10 She has to stop for breath 2,2

Who said that?

1 Puck 2,1
2 Oberon 2,1
3 Titania 2,1
4 Helena to Demetrius 2,1
5 Lysander to the sleeping Hermia 2,2

Open quotes

1 'And this same progeny of evils comes/From our debate, from our dissension.' 2,1
2 'They do square, that all their elves for fear/Creep into acorn cups and hide them there.' 2,1
3 'I know a bank where the wild thyme blows/Where oxlips and the nodding violet grows.' 2,1
4 'When thou wak'st, it is thy dear./Wake when some vile thing is near.' 2,2
5 'The will of man is by his reason sway'd/And reason says you are the worthier maid.' 2,2

Connections

1 Oberon is accused of loving Hippolyta, and Titania of loving Theseus 2,1
2 Lion, bear, wolf, bull, monkey or ape, ounce, cat, pard, boar. It is actually an 'ass': Bottom 2,1 2,2
3 She means that Demetrius is all the company she needs. There are indeed others in the wood 2,1
4 Titania will be tormented. Demetrius will love Helena and she will fly from him 2,1
5 Hermia had to choose between her love for Lysander and death, in Athens 2,2

Natural and magical

1 Oberon sees Cupid. Oberon and Titania are 'ill met'. Titania and her fairies 'revel' 2,1
2 A mermaid on a dolphin's back singing, so that the seas calmed and stars fell 2,1
3 A dove pursuing a griffin; a hind catching a tiger: images contrary to normal nature 2,1
4 Thyme, oxlips, violet, woodbine, musk-roses, eglantine. Wild, nodding, luscious, sweet 2,1
5 In Titania's bower, a snake sheds its skin to wrap a fairy in 2,1; 'Spotted snakes with double tongue' are charmed away from the sleeping Queen 2,2; Hermia dreams of a snake eating her heart away, with Lysander watching smiling 2,2

■ Self-test answers Act 3

Uncover the plot

Puck reports to Oberon on his pranks, including the fact that Titania loves Bottom, who has been given an ass's head during the play rehearsal. Meanwhile Demetrius has caught up with Hermia, who still spurns him, desperate to find Lysander.

Oberon realises that Demetrius has not been charmed as planned; he now charms him, as Helena enters, pursued by the enchanted Lysander. Demetrius wakes and also declares love for Helena. Hermia joins them, is distraught to find that Lysander hates her, and blames Helena. Meanwhile, Helena accuses all three of conspiring to bait her. As the men are about to fight, Oberon steps in: Puck separates them and, as all four lovers sleep, puts antidote juice on Lysander's eyes. With Oberon on his way to do the same for Titania, all will be put right.

Who? What? Where? Why? How?

1 Hermia is smaller, Helena taller. Hermia says: 'I am so dwarfish and so low./How low am I, thou painted maypole?' 3,2
2 Demetrius, so he loves Helena. This is right, because he should love her: as Oberon says, this is a case not of 'true love turned' (as when Lysander loved Helena) but of 'false turn'd true' 3,2
3 Pyramus' suicide and the lion being too realistic and frightening. How to make the moonlight and the wall realistic enough 3,1
4 Jewels from the sea, fruits, honey and wax candles lit by glow-worms, fans of butterfly wings 3,1
5 A spot 'near the cradle of the Fairy Queen' 3,1
6 At night, 'wand'ring here and there'. At dawn, 'home to churchyards' 3,2
7 To show the others he is not frightened: he wakes Titania, who falls in love with him 3,1
8 For still following her around. Because she can't believe Lysander would abandon her, and suspects Demetrius of having killed him 3,2
9 He gets Puck to bring dark and fog, to lead them away from each other by imitating their voices, and to exhaust them into sleep 3,2
10 As 'the shallowest thickskin of that barren sort' (the workmen) 3,2

Who said that?

1 Titania 3,1
2 Bottom. Titania's love is indeed not reasonable – and it is ironic that wisdom should come from Bottom who – more truly than he is aware – keeps calling himself an ass 3,1
3 Helena of Hermia. The repeated 'size' references enrage Hermia 3,2
4 Puck 3,2
5 Oberon 3,2

Open quotes

1 'I see their knavery. This is to make an ass of me; to fright me, if they could' 3,1
2 'Of thy misprision must perforce ensue/Some true love turn'd and not a false turned true.' 3,2
3 'You both are rivals, and love Hermia;/And now both rivals, to mock Helena' 3,2
4 'Even till the eastern gate all fiery red,/Opening on Neptune with fair blessed beams/Turns into yellow gold his salt green streams.' 3,2
5 'Jack shall have Jill,/Nought shall go ill.' 3,2

Connections

1 Illusion in the workmen's play (ill understood by them) 3,1; the men's illusory love for Helena. Titania's illusory passion for Bottom 3,2
2 That there is a deliberate conspiracy to torment them 3,1 3,2
3 Demetrius: exhausted by sorrow; Lysander and Demetrius (again): exhausted from the chase; Helena: to escape her sorrow; Hermia: faintness 3,2
4 Titania, because of Bottom's singing: to fall in love with him. 3,1; Demetrius, because of Hermia and Lysander's arguing: to fall in love with Helena 3,2

5 Oberon and Titania have also 'met by moonlight'; Lysander has told Helena 'Reason says you are the worthier maid' (untrue to his real feelings, like Titania); Theseus earlier connected the moon to the enforced chastity of a nun

Contrasts
1 'And I will purge thy mortal grossness so/That thou shalt like an airy spirit go' 3,1
2 Bottom is given food, light, bedding, etc. 3,1; Workmen: 'briars and thorns at their apparel snatch;' Hermia is 'Bedabbled with the dew, and torn with briars.' 3,2
3 'O Helen, goddess, nymph, perfect, divine!' (Rather different language!) 3,2
4 She was a vixen when she went to school 3,2
5 Ghosts/damned spirits who 'must for aye consort with black-brow'd night' and 'spirits of another sort', who 'with the Morning's love have oft made sport' 3,2

▪ Self-test answers Act 4

Uncover the plot
Titania and Bottom settle close by the sleeping lovers. Oberon has already met her and been given the child he wanted, and now wants peace. Oberon releases Titania, who, waking, loathes Bottom's face, while Puck removes the ass's head. The five sleepers are charmed deeper, as the fairies dance and depart, resolving to bless the festivities in Athens the following midnight. Theseus and Hippolyta arrive to hunt with hounds and wake the lovers. Lysander confesses the elopement plan, Egeus demands punishment, but Demetrius confesses his change of heart: Theseus rules that all shall be married. Bottom wakes alone, and hurries to join the players.

Who? What? Where? Why? How?
1 The four lovers and Bottom: Titania, the sixth sleeper, is already awake 4,1
2 To Theseus for law: he is overruled. To Demetrius for backup: Demetrius says he has changed his mind 4,1
3 Being 'marvellous hairy about the face', and hungry for oats and hay 4,1
4 'When my cue comes, call me, and I will answer.' 4,1
5 To the same place where the four lovers are asleep 4,1
6 In Athens. Back to purely human concerns: it is also daytime, and the language is prose 4,2
7 He feels sorry for her, and has been given the changeling he wanted 4,1
8 Though they are slow, their barking is particularly musical 4,1
9 With joy: they were to make their fortune by the play, and couldn't do it without Bottom 4,2
10 As a sick man, off his food, coming back to his natural appetite 4,1

Who said that?
1 Demetrius 4,1
2 Egeus of Demetrius 4,1
3 Bottom 4,1
4 Oberon 4,1
5 Quince of Bottom. He means 'paragon' 4,2

Open quotes

1 'So doth the woodbine the sweet honeysuckle/Gently entwist; the female ivy so/Enrings the barky fingers of the elm' 4,1

2 'How comes this gentle concord in the world/That hatred is so far from jealousy/To sleep by hate and fear no enmity?' 4,1

3 'For she his hairy temples then had rounded/With coronet of fresh and fragrant flowers' 4,1

4 'These things seem small and undistinguishable,/Like far-off mountains turned into clouds.' 4,1

5 'For we are to utter sweet breath; and I doubt not but to hear them say it is a sweet comedy' 4,2

Connections

1 Oberon's speech beginning: 'Now thou and I are new in amity...' (line 84) Titania and Oberon are together; so are the lovers; they will meet at the royal wedding; the 'jollity' will be provided by the players 4,1

2 The royal wedding and the workmen's play

3 Oberon says that everyone will think of the events 'But as the fierce vexation of a dream'; Titania thinks she has had a 'vision'; Demetrius says the lovers feel they are still dreaming; Bottom thinks he has dreamt everything 4,1

4 Bottom's request for 'the tongs and the bones'; music to charm sleep; music of the hounds; Bottom's plan for a ballad of his dream 4,1

Called to order

1 To undo confusion: Puck removes Bottom's ass head; Oberon releases Titania; The lovers are given sleep 4,1

2 Theseus and daylight. This establishes order – mortal power – instead of fairy rule 4,1

3 They use formal, courteous titles: Fairy King, My Queen, My Lord, etc. 4,1

4 They progress from 'musical confusion' to 'so musical a discord' to 'match'd in mouth' and 'tuneable': becoming progressively harmonious 4,1

5 The matched couples are called 'three and three' (three being a number symbolic of order); the return to Athens is heralded; a 'solemn' feast is awaited 4,1

◼ Self-test answers Act 5

Uncover the plot

Theseus thinks the lovers' story a fantasy, but Hippolyta is not so sure. The couples meet after supper and are offered a list of four entertainments. Despite Philostrate's warnings, Theseus chooses Pyramus and Thisbe, because it is sincerely offered. Quince delivers a garbled Prologue, and the play proceeds with wry commentary by Theseus and Demetrius. Thisbe's mantle is mauled by the lion, Pyramus, finding it, stabs himself, and Thisbe (played by Flute), discovering him dead, does likewise. After a final bergomask, the players depart and the others retire. The fairies come to bless the place, and the last word is left to Puck.

Who? What? Where? Why? How?

1 Master of the Revels

2 Quince and Puck

3 A wall

4 They both apologise to the audience for any offence
5 In the lantern: the lantern is the moon, and he is the man in the moon. There is a lit candle inside
6 All round the palace. Titania and Oberon bless the royal chamber
7 Because they each tell the same story
8 They were tears of laughter
9 'A tedious brief scene of young Pyramus and his love Thisbe, very tragical mirth.'
10 'Hard-handed men that work in Athens here,/Which never labour'd in their minds til now.'

Who said that?
1 Theseus. The fairies were indeed involved
2 Theseus
3 Hippolyta
4 Bottom. He is inturrupting and taking literally remarks by Theseus and Demetrius; he is out of character – and, moreover, supposed to be dead!
5 Puck. Applaud

Open quotes
1 'The lunatic, the lover and the poet/Are of imagination all compact.'
2 'Whereat with blade, with bloody blameful blade,/He bravely broach'd his boiling bloody breast'
3 'Lovers to bed: tis almost fairy time.'
4 'And each several chamber bless/Through this palace, with sweet peace'
5 'If we shadows have offended/Think but this and all is mended/That you have but slumbered here/While these vision did appear.'

Connections
1 The girls were abandoned in the wood, in danger from wild beasts. The players feel bound to warn them that Snug is not a real lion, in case they are afraid!
2 Bottom has indeed been an ass!
3 Hermia, Lysander and Demetrius have all risked death for love
4 The fairies danced before leaving, and do so again in the palace
5 Puck delivers an epilogue at the end of the play as a whole: as a fairy, he is a more appropriate commentator on illusion and reality
6 The fairy world has come into the mortal palace – as predicted earlier by the players, who nevertheless felt the need to 'fake' it.

General questions on the play
1 Helena and Demetrius; Hermia and Lysander loved each other
   Demetrius and Lysander both love Hermia
   Demetrius and Lysander both love Helena
   Back to square one
2 L Love
   O Order
   W Wood, waking
   M Moon, music, madness, marriage, magic
   I Infatuation, illusion, imagination
   N Nature
   D Dreams, discord, dancing, darkness
   S Sleep, singing, serpents